Expectation

Unleashing the Power of Expectation: How to Transform Your Mindset, Achieve Your Goals, and Live Your Best Life with Proven Self-Help Strategies and Practical Exercises to Create the Future You Desire

Lance P. Richards

I0625380

Expectation: Unleashing the Power of Expectation: How to Transform Your Mindset, Achieve Your Goals, and Live Your Best Life with Proven Self-Help Strategies and Practical Exercises to Create the Future You Desire

Table of Contents

01: Introduction: Understanding the Power of Expectation

Introduction:

Expectation is a powerful force that can shape our lives in profound ways. It is the belief that something will happen or come to fruition in the future. Expectation can be positive or negative, and it can influence our thoughts, emotions, and behaviors. The power of expectation lies in its ability to create a self-fulfilling prophecy. When we expect something to happen, we tend to act in ways that make it more likely to happen, whether consciously or unconsciously. In this way, expectation can either help us achieve our goals or hold us back from reaching our full potential.

The concept of expectation is not a new one. Throughout history, people have recognized the power of expectation and have used it to their advantage. From ancient cultures who used rituals and ceremonies to manifest their desires to modern-day self-help gurus who teach visualization and affirmations, the power of expectation has been harnessed by many.

The question is, how can we use the power of expectation to

01: INTRODUCTION: UNDERSTANDING THE POWER OF EXPECTATION

transform our lives and achieve our goals? The answer lies in understanding how expectation works and how to cultivate positive expectations that support our desires.

The Science of Expectation:

Expectation is not just a spiritual or mystical concept; it is also a scientific one. Research has shown that our expectations can influence our perception, behavior, and even our physical health. When we expect something to happen, our brain releases chemicals that prepare us for that event. For example, if we expect to experience pain, our brain will release chemicals that increase our sensitivity to pain. On the other hand, if we expect to experience pleasure, our brain will release chemicals that make us more receptive to pleasure.

This phenomenon is known as the placebo effect, and it has been studied extensively in medicine. The placebo effect occurs when a person experiences a positive outcome after receiving a treatment that has no therapeutic effect. This effect is thought to be due to the power of expectation. When a person expects to feel better, their brain releases chemicals that promote healing, even if the treatment they received has no real medicinal value.

The placebo effect is not limited to medicine. It can also be observed in other areas of life, such as sports, business, and education. For example, studies have shown that students who are told they are smart tend to perform better academically than those who are told they are not. Similarly, athletes who are told they are talented tend to perform better than those who are told they are not.

The Role of Beliefs:

Beliefs are an essential component of expectation. Our beliefs shape our expectations, and our expectations, in turn, shape our reality. If we believe that we are capable of achieving our goals, we are more likely to take action that supports that belief. If we believe that we are not capable, we are more likely to give up before we even try.

Beliefs can be positive or negative, and they are often formed based on our past experiences, upbringing, and social conditioning. For example, if we grew up in an environment where success was celebrated, we are more likely to have positive beliefs about our ability to achieve success.

Conversely, if we grew up in an environment where failure was punished, we are more likely to have negative beliefs about our ability to succeed.

The good news is that beliefs can be changed. Through self-reflection, education, and experience, we can challenge and modify our beliefs to support our desires. This process is not always easy, but it is necessary if we want to unleash the power of expectation in our lives.

The Importance of Mindset:

Our mindset is the lens through which we view the world. It is the set of beliefs, attitudes, and expectations that shape our thoughts and behaviors. Our mindset can either support our desires or hold us back from achieving them.

There are two main types of mindsets: a fixed mindset and a growth mindset. A fixed mindset is the belief that our abilities and talents are fixed and cannot be changed. This mindset can lead to a fear of failure, a lack of motivation, and a reluctance to take risks. On the other hand, a growth mindset is the belief that our abilities and talents can be developed through hard work, persistence, and learning. This mindset encourages us to embrace challenges, learn from failure, and strive for improvement.

The good news is that we can cultivate a growth mindset through intentional effort and practice. By focusing on our strengths, setting realistic goals, and embracing challenges, we can shift our mindset from fixed to growth and unleash the power of expectation in our lives.

Practical Strategies for Cultivating Positive Expectations:

Identify your limiting beliefs: The first step in cultivating positive expectations is to identify the limiting beliefs that are holding you back. These beliefs may be conscious or unconscious, but they are likely rooted in past experiences, social conditioning, or self-doubt. Once you have identified your limiting beliefs, challenge them by asking yourself if they are true, where they come from, and how they are holding you back.

Practice visualization: Visualization is a powerful tool for cultivating positive expectations. It involves using your imagination to create vivid mental images of the future you desire. By visualizing your desired outcome, you can create a positive expectation that supports your goals. To practice visualization, find a quiet place where you can focus and imagine yourself achieving your desired outcome in detail.

Affirmations: Affirmations are positive statements that reinforce positive expectations. By repeating affirmations, you can shift your mindset and cultivate positive expectations. To create effective affirmations, focus on your desired outcome, use positive language, and repeat them often.

Gratitude: Gratitude is a powerful tool for cultivating positive expectations. By focusing on what you are grateful for, you can shift your mindset from scarcity to abundance. When you feel grateful, you are more likely to expect positive outcomes and take actions that support your desires.

Conclusion:

Expectation is a powerful force that can shape our lives in profound ways. By understanding how expectation works and cultivating positive expectations, we can transform our mindset, achieve our goals, and live our best lives. The key is to identify our limiting beliefs, cultivate a growth mindset, and practice practical strategies that support positive

01: INTRODUCTION: UNDERSTANDING THE POWER OF EXPECTATION

expectations. With intention and effort, we can unleash the power of expectation and create the future we desire.

02: The Science behind Expectation: How It Shapes Your Reality

Expectation is a powerful force that can shape our reality in profound ways. Our beliefs and expectations influence not only how we perceive the world but also how we act and react to it. In this chapter, we will explore the science behind expectation and how it shapes our reality.

The Power of Perception:

Perception is the process of interpreting sensory information to create a meaningful experience. Our perception is shaped by our beliefs, expectations, and past experiences. In other words, what we perceive is not solely determined by what is happening in the external world but also by our internal world.

For example, imagine that you are walking down a dark alley at night. If you believe that the alley is dangerous and that you are likely to be attacked, your perception of the alley will be different than if you believe that the alley is safe and that nothing bad will happen. Your expectation shapes your perception, and your perception shapes your reality.

02: THE SCIENCE BEHIND EXPECTATION: HOW IT SHAPES YOUR REALITY

The Brain and Expectation:

Our expectations are not just thoughts or beliefs; they are also physical experiences in the brain. The brain has a network of neurons that are activated when we experience something and when we imagine or expect something. This means that when we expect something to happen, our brain prepares for that event as if it were already happening.

For example, if you are expecting to eat a piece of chocolate, your brain will release dopamine, a neurotransmitter associated with pleasure, before you even take a bite. This means that your expectation of pleasure actually triggers a physical response in your brain, shaping your reality and your experience.

The Placebo Effect:

The placebo effect is a well-known phenomenon in medicine, where a person is given a treatment that has no therapeutic effect, yet they experience an improvement in their symptoms. The placebo effect is a powerful demonstration of the power of expectation in shaping our reality.

02: THE SCIENCE BEHIND EXPECTATION: HOW IT SHAPES YOUR REALITY

The placebo effect works because our expectations can trigger physical responses in the brain and body. For example, if you expect a sugar pill to reduce your pain, your brain may release endorphins, natural painkillers, in response to that expectation, reducing your perception of pain.

The Pygmalion Effect:

The Pygmalion effect is a phenomenon where higher expectations lead to an increase in performance. In other words, if you expect someone to perform well, they are more likely to perform well, and if you expect someone to perform poorly, they are more likely to perform poorly.

The Pygmalion effect has been demonstrated in many different contexts, from academic performance to athletic performance to job performance. It works because our expectations influence our beliefs about our own abilities and our motivation to succeed.

How to Harness the Power of Expectation:

Now that we understand the science behind expectation, how can we harness its power to shape our reality? Here are some practical strategies:

Set high expectations: Set high expectations for yourself and others. Believe that you can achieve your goals and that others can achieve theirs. This will increase motivation and performance.

Visualize success: Visualize yourself succeeding in your goals. This will create a positive expectation that supports your actions.

Surround yourself with positive influences: Surround yourself with people who have positive expectations for you and who support your goals. This will reinforce your positive expectations and motivate you to succeed.

Focus on the present: Focus on the present moment and on what you can do right now to achieve your goals. This will help you to take action and avoid getting bogged down by negative expectations.

Conclusion:

Expectation is a powerful force that shapes our reality in profound ways. Our beliefs and expectations influence not only how we perceive the world but also how we act and re-act to it. By understanding the science behind expectation and harnessing its power, we can create a positive reality that supports our goals and helps us to live our best lives.

03: Overcoming Limiting Beliefs and Embracing Positive Expectations

Limiting beliefs can hold us back from achieving our goals and living our best lives. They are the negative thoughts and beliefs that we have about ourselves, others, and the world around us. These beliefs can be deeply ingrained and difficult to change, but with the power of positive expectations, we can overcome them and transform our mindset. In this chapter, we will explore how to overcome limiting beliefs and embrace positive expectations.

Understanding Limiting Beliefs:

Limiting beliefs are beliefs that we hold about ourselves, others, or the world that are not necessarily true but that we believe to be true. These beliefs can be self-imposed or imposed by external factors such as family, culture, or society.

Limiting beliefs can manifest in different areas of our lives, such as our relationships, career, finances, and health. For example, if we believe that we are not good enough to pursue a certain career, we may limit ourselves by not even trying to pursue it.

03: OVERCOMING LIMITING BELIEFS AND EMBRA-CING POSITIVE EXPECTATIONS

Overcoming Limiting Beliefs:

Overcoming limiting beliefs requires a willingness to challenge and question them. It also requires a shift in mindset from a fixed mindset to a growth mindset.

Here are some practical strategies for overcoming limiting beliefs:

Identify your limiting beliefs: The first step in overcoming limiting beliefs is to identify them. Write down the negative thoughts and beliefs that you have about yourself, others, or the world around you.

Challenge your limiting beliefs: Once you have identified your limiting beliefs, challenge them by asking yourself if they are really true. Look for evidence that contradicts your beliefs and consider alternative perspectives.

Reframe your beliefs: Reframe your beliefs by replacing negative thoughts with positive ones. For example, instead of thinking "I'm not good enough to pursue my dream career," reframe it as "I have the skills and potential to pursue my dream career."

03: OVERCOMING LIMITING BELIEFS AND EMBRA-
CING POSITIVE EXPECTATIONS

Take action: Take action towards your goals, even if it feels uncomfortable or challenging. This will help you to build confidence and challenge your limiting beliefs.

Embracing Positive Expectations:

Positive expectations are beliefs that support our goals and desires. They are the beliefs that we have about ourselves, others, and the world that are positive and supportive. Embracing positive expectations can help us to overcome limiting beliefs and transform our mindset.

Here are some practical strategies for embracing positive expectations:

Visualize success: Visualize yourself succeeding in your goals. This will create a positive expectation that supports your actions.

Practice positive self-talk: Practice positive self-talk by using affirmations and positive statements about yourself. For example, say "I am capable of achieving my goals" instead of "I am not good enough."

Surround yourself with positive influences: Surround yourself with people who have positive expectations for you and who support your goals. This will reinforce your positive expectations and motivate you to succeed.

Celebrate your successes: Celebrate your successes, no matter how small they may be. This will reinforce your positive expectations and help you to build confidence.

Conclusion:

Overcoming limiting beliefs and embracing positive expectations is essential for transforming your mindset and achieving your goals. By challenging your negative beliefs and replacing them with positive ones, you can shift from a fixed mindset to a growth mindset. Embracing positive expectations will support your goals and desires and help you to live your best life. With the power of expectation, you can overcome your limiting beliefs and create the future you desire.

04: How to Set Goals and Expectations that Align with Your Values

In order to live a fulfilling life and achieve success, it is important to set goals and expectations that align with your values. Your values are the principles and beliefs that guide your behavior and decisions. When you align your goals and expectations with your values, you are more likely to feel fulfilled and satisfied with your accomplishments. In this chapter, we will explore how to set goals and expectations that align with your values.

Identifying Your Values:

The first step in setting goals and expectations that align with your values is to identify your values. Your values are unique to you and may change over time. To identify your values, ask yourself the following questions:

– What is important to me in life?

– What principles do I live by?

– What beliefs guide my behavior and decisions?

– What do I want to be remembered for?

04: HOW TO SET GOALS AND EXPECTATIONS THAT ALIGN WITH YOUR VALUES

Once you have identified your values, write them down and use them as a guide for setting goals and expectations.

Setting SMART Goals:

SMART goals are specific, measurable, achievable, relevant, and time-bound. By setting SMART goals, you are more likely to achieve them and stay motivated. Here are the key components of SMART goals:

– Specific: Your goal should be clear and specific. For example, instead of setting a goal to "lose weight," set a goal to "lose 10 pounds in three months."

– Measurable: Your goal should be measurable so that you can track your progress. For example, you can measure your weight loss progress by weighing yourself regularly.

– Achievable: Your goal should be achievable so that you do not feel overwhelmed or discouraged. For example, setting a goal to lose 50 pounds in one month is not achievable and may lead to failure.

– Relevant: Your goal should be relevant to your values and aligned with your overall vision for your life. For example, if your value is health, setting a goal to improve your fitness level is relevant.

– Time-bound: Your goal should have a deadline so that you can stay motivated and focused. For example, setting a deadline to achieve your weight loss goal in three months will help you stay on track.

Aligning Your Goals with Your Values:

Once you have set SMART goals, it is important to ensure that they align with your values. Here are some strategies for aligning your goals with your values:

Review your values: Review your values regularly and ensure that your goals are aligned with them. If a goal does not align with your values, it may not be worth pursuing.

Set goals that support your vision: Your goals should support your overall vision for your life. If your vision is to live a healthy lifestyle, set goals that support that vision, such as exercising regularly and eating a balanced diet.

Prioritize your goals: Prioritize your goals based on their importance to your values and vision. Focus on the goals that align most closely with your values.

Re-evaluate your goals regularly: Re-evaluate your goals regularly and adjust them as needed. As your values and vision may change over time, it is important to ensure that your goals are still relevant.

Creating Positive Expectations:

Creating positive expectations is key to achieving your goals and living a fulfilling life. Positive expectations are the beliefs that you have about yourself and your ability to achieve your goals. Here are some strategies for creating positive expectations:

Visualize success: Visualize yourself achieving your goals and living the life you want. This will create a positive expectation that supports your actions.

Practice positive self-talk: Practice positive self-talk by using affirmations and positive statements about yourself. For example, say "I am capable of achieving my goals" instead of "I am not good enough."

Celebrate your successes: Celebrate your successes, no matter how small they may be. This will reinforce your positive expectations and motivate you to keep going.

Surround yourself with positivity: Surround yourself with positive people and environments. Negative people and environments can undermine your positive expectations and derail your progress.

Focus on your strengths: Focus on your strengths and use them to achieve your goals. This will build your confidence and reinforce your positive expectations.

Learn from failures: Instead of viewing failures as setbacks, view them as opportunities to learn and grow. This will help you maintain a positive attitude and continue to expect success.

Conclusion:

Setting goals and expectations that align with your values is essential for living a fulfilling life and achieving success. By using the strategies outlined in this chapter, you can set SMART goals, align them with your values, and create positive expectations that support your actions. Remember to regularly review and adjust your goals and expectations as needed, and celebrate your successes along the way. With the power of expectation on your side, you can create the future you desire and live your best life.

05: Building a Strong Mindset: Developing Mental Toughness and Resilience

Introduction:

Building a strong mindset is essential for achieving success in any area of life. A strong mindset allows you to overcome obstacles, persevere through challenges, and maintain a positive attitude even in the face of adversity. In this chapter, we will explore the concept of mental toughness and resilience and provide practical strategies and exercises to help you develop a strong mindset.

Understanding Mental Toughness and Resilience:

Mental toughness and resilience are closely related concepts that refer to the ability to withstand stress, overcome adversity, and bounce back from setbacks. Mental toughness involves developing a strong and disciplined mindset that enables you to stay focused and motivated even in difficult situations. Resilience, on the other hand, involves the ability to adapt and recover quickly from challenges and setbacks.

Developing Mental Toughness and Resilience:

05: BUILDING A STRONG MINDSET: DEVELOPING MENTAL TOUGHNESS AND RESILIENCE

Practice self-discipline: Developing mental toughness requires a high level of self-discipline. This means setting clear goals, developing a plan to achieve them, and sticking to it even when faced with distractions or setbacks.

Embrace challenges: Embracing challenges is an essential part of building mental toughness and resilience. Rather than avoiding challenges, seek out opportunities to test and strengthen your skills and abilities.

Adopt a growth mindset: A growth mindset is the belief that your abilities can be developed through hard work and dedication. By adopting a growth mindset, you can overcome self-doubt and maintain a positive attitude even when facing challenges.

Practice visualization: Visualization is a powerful tool for developing mental toughness and resilience. By visualizing yourself overcoming challenges and achieving success, you can reinforce positive expectations and increase your motivation and confidence.

Focus on the present moment: Maintaining a focus on the present moment can help you stay grounded and focused, even when facing stressful or challenging situations. This can help you avoid becoming overwhelmed or distracted by negative thoughts or emotions.

Cultivate a positive attitude: Cultivating a positive attitude is essential for developing mental toughness and resilience. This means focusing on the positive aspects of situations, reframing negative thoughts, and using positive self-talk to reinforce your confidence and motivation.

Practical Exercises for Developing Mental Toughness and Resilience:

Set challenging goals: Setting challenging goals can help you develop mental toughness and resilience by pushing you out of your comfort zone and forcing you to overcome obstacles and setbacks.

Practice meditation: Meditation is a powerful tool for developing mental toughness and resilience. By practicing mindfulness meditation, you can learn to focus your attention, regulate your emotions, and maintain a sense of calm even in stressful situations.

05: BUILDING A STRONG MINDSET: DEVELOPING MENTAL TOUGHNESS AND RESILIENCE

Challenge your beliefs: Challenging your beliefs can help you overcome self-doubt and build mental toughness and resilience. This means questioning negative self-talk, reframing negative thoughts, and focusing on your strengths and accomplishments.

Seek out positive role models: Seeking out positive role models can provide inspiration and motivation for developing mental toughness and resilience. This may involve finding mentors, reading biographies of successful people, or joining a supportive community of like-minded individuals.

Conclusion:

Building a strong mindset is essential for achieving success in any area of life. By developing mental toughness and resilience, you can overcome obstacles, persevere through challenges, and maintain a positive attitude even in the face of adversity. By practicing the strategies and exercises outlined in this chapter, you can develop a strong mindset that supports your goals and helps you create the future you desire. Remember to be patient, persistent, and kind to yourself along the way, and celebrate your successes no matter how small. With a strong mindset on your side, you can achieve

05: BUILDING A STRONG MINDSET: DEVELOPING MENTAL TOUGHNESS AND RESILIENCE

anything you set your mind to.

06: The Importance of Self-Talk: Shifting Your Internal Dialogue to Support Your Goals

Introduction

The way we talk to ourselves can have a profound impact on our ability to achieve our goals and live our best lives. Negative self-talk can hold us back and prevent us from reaching our full potential, while positive self-talk can help us build confidence, motivation, and resilience. In this chapter, we will explore the importance of self-talk, how it affects our mindset, and how we can shift our internal dialogue to support our goals.

The Power of Self-Talk

Our self-talk is the internal dialogue we have with ourselves throughout the day. It can be positive or negative, and it can have a significant impact on our thoughts, feelings, and behaviors. Research has shown that the way we talk to ourselves can affect our confidence, motivation, and even our physical health.

Negative self-talk, such as "I'm not good enough," "I can't

do this," or "I always mess up," can be damaging to our self-esteem and confidence. It can create a self-fulfilling prophecy, where we believe we will fail before we even try. On the other hand, positive self-talk, such as "I am capable," "I will succeed," or "I am confident," can build our self-esteem and motivate us to take action towards our goals.

Shifting Your Internal Dialogue

Changing your self-talk may seem like a daunting task, but it is possible with practice and persistence. Here are some strategies to help you shift your internal dialogue and support your goals:

Identify Your Negative Self-Talk: The first step to changing your self-talk is to become aware of your internal dialogue. Start paying attention to the thoughts that come up when you face challenges or setbacks. Write them down and identify the negative beliefs that underlie them.

Challenge Your Negative Beliefs: Once you have identified your negative self-talk, challenge the beliefs that underlie them. Ask yourself if they are true, and if there is any evidence to support them. Often, our negative beliefs are based on past experiences or self-doubt, rather than reality.

Reframe Your Negative Self-Talk: Once you have challenged
your negative beliefs, reframe your self-talk into positive
statements. For example, instead of saying "I can't do this,"
say "I am capable of figuring this out." Instead of saying "I
always mess up," say "I am learning and improving every
day."

Use Affirmations: Affirmations are positive statements that
you repeat to yourself to build confidence and motivation.
Choose affirmations that align with your goals and values
and repeat them to yourself regularly. For example, "I am
confident in my abilities," or "I am worthy of success."

Practice Gratitude: Gratitude can help shift your focus from
negative self-talk to positive self-talk. Take time each day to
reflect on the things you are grateful for, and focus on the
positive aspects of your life. This can help you build a more
positive mindset and support your goals.

Conclusion

The way we talk to ourselves can have a profound impact on

our mindset, our behaviors, and our ability to achieve our goals. Negative self-talk can hold us back and prevent us from reaching our full potential, while positive self-talk can build confidence, motivation, and resilience. By becoming aware of our internal dialogue, challenging our negative beliefs, and reframing our self-talk into positive statements, we can shift our mindset and support our goals.

07: How to Visualize Your Future and Use Imagery to Fuel Your Expectations

Introduction

Have you ever heard the saying "you need to see it to believe it?" When it comes to expectations, visualization is a powerful tool that can help you create the reality you desire. By visualizing your future and the outcomes you want to achieve, you can strengthen your expectations and increase your chances of success. In this chapter, we'll explore the science behind visualization, how to use it effectively, and some practical exercises to help you get started.

The Science of Visualization

Visualization is the process of creating a mental image or representation of a desired outcome. It's based on the idea that the mind and body are connected, and that our thoughts and beliefs can influence our physical reality. When we visualize a positive outcome, our brains release the same neurotransmitters as if we were actually experiencing that outcome. This can help us feel more motivated, confident, and focused, and can also improve our performance.

Studies have shown that visualization can be a powerful tool for achieving goals in a variety of fields, from sports to business to health. For example, athletes who use visualization techniques have been shown to improve their performance, reduce anxiety, and recover from injuries more quickly. In business, visualization can help entrepreneurs and executives clarify their goals and strategies, and can also help them communicate their vision to others. And in health, visualization has been used to manage pain, reduce stress, and improve the outcomes of medical treatments.

How to Visualize Your Future

To use visualization effectively, it's important to follow a few key steps:

Set a clear goal: Before you can visualize your desired outcome, you need to know what it is. Make sure your goal is specific, measurable, and achievable, and that it aligns with your values and expectations.

Create a mental image: Once you have a clear goal in mind,

close your eyes and create a mental image of what it will look and feel like when you achieve it. Imagine the details of the situation, including sights, sounds, smells, and emotions. Make the image as vivid and detailed as possible.

Engage your senses: As you visualize your desired outcome, try to engage all of your senses. What does it feel like to be there? What does it smell like? What sounds can you hear? The more sensory information you include, the more real your visualization will feel.

Stay positive: As you visualize your desired outcome, focus on the positive aspects of the situation. Visualize yourself succeeding, feeling confident, and enjoying the experience. Avoid negative self-talk or doubts that could undermine your expectations.

Repeat and reinforce: Visualization is a skill that takes practice to develop. Try to visualize your desired outcome on a regular basis, ideally daily. You can also reinforce your expectations by using positive affirmations or creating a vision board that includes images and words that represent your goals.

07: HOW TO VISUALIZE YOUR FUTURE AND USE IMAGERY TO FUEL YOUR EXPECTATIONS

Practical Exercises

Here are some practical exercises to help you develop your visualization skills:

Guided visualization: You can find many guided visualization exercises online or in books. These exercises will walk you through the process of creating a mental image of your desired outcome, step by step. Some guided visualizations are specific to certain goals or situations, such as sports performance or public speaking, while others are more general.

Imagery rehearsal: This technique is commonly used in sports psychology to help athletes prepare for competition. It involves visualizing a specific scenario or performance, such as a race or game, in detail. By rehearsing the scenario mentally, athletes can improve their confidence and performance.

Vision board: A vision board is a visual representation of your goals and desires. It can include images, words, and symbols that represent your desired outcomes. Creating a vision board can help you clarify your goals, reinforce your expectations, and stay motivated.

07: HOW TO VISUALIZE YOUR FUTURE AND USE IMAGERY TO FUEL YOUR EXPECTATIONS

Once you have created your visualization, it's important to focus on the emotions and feelings that come with it. Visualizing alone isn't enough to create the future you desire; you must also attach strong emotions to it. Your emotions play a crucial role in shaping your expectations and driving your actions.

As you visualize your future, ask yourself how it will make you feel when you achieve it. Will you feel proud, accomplished, happy, or fulfilled? Once you have identified the emotions that come with your visualization, focus on them and let them sink in. Imagine yourself already experiencing those emotions, as if you have already achieved your goal.

Using positive affirmations can also help reinforce your visualization and strengthen your expectations. These are short, positive statements that you repeat to yourself daily, such as "I am capable of achieving my goals" or "I believe in myself and my abilities." The more you repeat these affirmations, the more you will start to internalize them and believe them to be true.

In addition to visualizing and affirmations, creating a vision board can also help to fuel your expectations. A vision board is a visual representation of your goals and aspirations. It can include pictures, quotes, and symbols that represent the things you want to achieve. By looking at your vision board every day, you will keep your goals at the forefront of your mind and remind yourself of what you are working towards.

It's important to note that visualization and imagery should not be used as a substitute for action. While visualizing and affirming your goals can help you to believe in yourself and your abilities, you must also take concrete steps towards achieving your goals. Use your visualization and positive self-talk to fuel your motivation and drive your actions.

In summary, visualization and imagery can be powerful tools in creating and fueling your expectations. By creating a clear picture of your desired future and attaching strong emotions to it, you can shape your expectations and drive your actions towards achieving your goals. Combining visualization with positive affirmations and creating a vision board can also help to reinforce your expectations and keep your goals at the forefront of your mind. Remember, however, that visualization and positive self-talk should be used in conjunction with action towards your goals.

08: The Role of Emotion in Expectation: Harnessing Your Feelings to Create Positive Outcomes

Emotions are an integral part of human nature. They are what make us feel alive and experience the world around us in a meaningful way. When it comes to expectation, emotions play a crucial role in shaping our beliefs, actions, and outcomes. In this chapter, we will explore the importance of emotions in expectation and how we can harness them to create positive outcomes.

Emotions and Expectation

Expectation is not just a cognitive process, but an emotional one as well. Our beliefs about what we can achieve and how we can achieve it are deeply tied to our emotions. If we feel anxious or fearful about a particular outcome, we may be less likely to pursue it, while positive emotions such as excitement or enthusiasm can motivate us to take action.

Moreover, our emotional state can influence the way we perceive and interpret events. For example, if we are in a negative emotional state, we may be more likely to perceive obstacles as insurmountable or setbacks as catastrophic. On the other hand, if we are in a positive emotional state, we may be more likely to see opportunities and possibilities in even the most challenging situations.

Therefore, it is important to manage our emotional state when it comes to expectation. By learning to regulate our emotions and cultivate positive feelings, we can create a more supportive environment for our expectations.

Emotional Intelligence and Expectation

Emotional intelligence is the ability to recognize, understand, and regulate one's emotions, as well as the emotions of others. It is a critical skill for effective communication, leadership, and relationship building, but it is also essential for expectation.

When it comes to expectation, emotional intelligence helps us to identify and manage our emotions. We can use it to recognize when our emotions are getting in the way of our expectations, and take steps to regulate them.

For example, if we feel anxious or doubtful about a particular outcome, we can use emotional intelligence to identify the root cause of those emotions. We may discover that our anxiety is driven by fear of failure or a lack of confidence in our abilities. With this awareness, we can then take steps to address those underlying issues, such as building our skills or seeking support from others.

Similarly, emotional intelligence can help us to cultivate positive emotions that support our expectations. By focusing on gratitude, joy, and optimism, we can create a more positive emotional environment that fuels our expectations and motivates us to take action.

Emotional Regulation Techniques

There are many techniques we can use to regulate our emotions and create a more supportive environment for our expectations. Here are a few examples:

Mindfulness - Mindfulness is the practice of being present and aware of our thoughts, feelings, and surroundings. By practicing mindfulness, we can learn to observe our emotions without judgment, and regulate them more effectively.

Breathing exercises - Deep breathing exercises can help to

calm our nervous system and reduce feelings of anxiety or stress.

Gratitude - Gratitude is a powerful emotion that can shift our focus from what we don't have to what we do have. By cultivating gratitude, we can create a more positive emotional environment that supports our expectations.

Positive self-talk - Positive self-talk involves using affirmations and positive statements to counteract negative self-talk. By focusing on positive statements such as "I can do this" or "I am capable," we can build our confidence and create a more positive emotional state.

Harnessing Positive Emotions

Positive emotions such as joy, excitement, and enthusiasm can be powerful tools for fueling our expectations. When we feel positive emotions, we are more likely to take action and pursue our goals with energy and enthusiasm.

Another way to harness emotions in expectation is through affirmations. Affirmations are positive statements that you repeat to yourself to affirm your desired outcome. By re-

08: THE ROLE OF EMOTION IN EXPECTATION: HARNESSING YOUR FEELINGS TO CREATE POSITIVE OUTCOMES

peating these affirmations, you are reinforcing your positive expectations and programming your subconscious mind to believe that your desired outcome is possible.

When creating affirmations, it's important to use positive, present tense language. For example, instead of saying "I will be successful," say "I am successful." This helps to create a sense of already having achieved your desired outcome, which can help to boost your confidence and motivation.

Another way to use emotions in expectation is through the power of gratitude. When you focus on what you are grateful for, you are naturally raising your vibration and opening yourself up to positive outcomes. By expressing gratitude for what you have now, you are signaling to the universe that you are ready to receive even more abundance and success.

Finally, it's important to remember that expectation is not a one-time event. It's an ongoing process that requires regular attention and practice. By staying committed to your positive expectations and taking consistent action towards

08: THE ROLE OF EMOTION IN EXPECTATION: HARNESSING YOUR FEELINGS TO CREATE POSITIVE OUTCOMES

your goals, you can create the future that you desire.

In conclusion, the role of emotions in expectation cannot be overstated. By harnessing the power of positive emotions, we can create a mindset that supports our goals and helps us to achieve our dreams. Through visualization, affirmations, gratitude, and consistent action, we can transform our expectations and unleash the power of expectation in our lives.

09: The Power of Affirmations: Using Positive Statements to Reinforce Your Expectations

The power of affirmations is one of the most effective ways to reinforce your expectations and manifest your desired outcomes. Affirmations are positive statements that you repeat to yourself to change your mindset and beliefs. By consistently reciting affirmations, you can reprogram your subconscious mind and change your thoughts, emotions, and actions.

Affirmations can help you overcome negative beliefs and self-doubt that may be holding you back from achieving your goals. They can help you build confidence, self-esteem, and resilience. When you focus on positive statements, you create a shift in your perception and attitude towards life. You begin to see things in a new light and approach challenges with a positive mindset.

To use affirmations effectively, it is important to create a list of positive statements that resonate with your goals and aspirations. The affirmations should be in the present tense, affirmative, and focused on what you want to achieve. For example, if your goal is to be more confident, your affirmation could be, "I am confident in myself and my abilities."

When reciting affirmations, it is important to do so with conviction and feeling. Repeat the affirmations several times a day, ideally in the morning and before going to bed. You can also write them down and place them where you can see them throughout the day, such as on your bathroom mirror or computer screen.

In addition to reciting affirmations, you can also use visualization techniques to reinforce your expectations. Visualize yourself achieving your goals and living the life you desire. See yourself in vivid detail, imagining the sights, sounds, and feelings associated with your success. The more vivid and detailed your visualization, the more powerful it will be.

It is important to remember that affirmations and visualization are not magic. They are tools to help you shift your mindset and reinforce your expectations. However, they must be accompanied by action. You must take steps towards your goals and put in the necessary work to achieve them. Affirmations and visualization can help you stay focused and motivated on your journey, but ultimately, you are responsible for making your dreams a reality.

In conclusion, the power of affirmations is a proven self-help strategy that can help you reinforce your expectations, shift your mindset, and achieve your goals. By consistently reciting positive statements and visualizing your success, you can create a shift in your perception and attitude towards life. Remember to accompany affirmations and visualization with action, and you will be well on your way to living the life you desire.

10: How to Practice Gratitude and Foster a Positive Attitude

Introduction:

Gratitude is the act of feeling thankful and appreciative for what you have in your life, both big and small. It is a powerful emotion that can have a significant impact on your overall well-being, happiness, and success. When you focus on the good things in your life and express gratitude for them, you create a positive attitude that can help you overcome challenges and achieve your goals. In this chapter, we will explore the benefits of practicing gratitude and offer practical tips on how to cultivate a positive attitude.

The Benefits of Gratitude:

Research has shown that practicing gratitude can have numerous positive effects on both your physical and mental health. When you express gratitude, it can:

Improve Your Mental Health: Gratitude has been linked to increased happiness, reduced depression and anxiety, and increased resilience in the face of stress and trauma.

Boost Your Physical Health: Practicing gratitude can improve your immune system, lower blood pressure, and reduce symptoms of chronic pain.

Strengthen Relationships: Grateful people tend to have stronger and more fulfilling relationships, as they are more likely to express appreciation and kindness towards others.

Increase Productivity: When you are grateful for what you have, you are more likely to be motivated and productive in your work and personal life.

Improve Sleep: Gratitude can help reduce the symptoms of insomnia, making it easier for you to get a good night's sleep.

How to Practice Gratitude:

Now that you understand the benefits of gratitude, let's explore some practical ways to incorporate it into your daily life.

Keep a Gratitude Journal: Writing down three things you are grateful for each day can help you focus on the good in your life and increase your feelings of positivity.

10: HOW TO PRACTICE GRATITUDE AND FOSTER A POSITIVE ATTITUDE

Express Gratitude to Others: Take the time to thank someone for something they did for you, whether it was big or small. It can be as simple as a handwritten note or a verbal expression of thanks.

Practice Mindfulness: Taking the time to be present in the moment and appreciate the little things in life can help cultivate a sense of gratitude.

Reframe Negative Thoughts: When you encounter negative thoughts, try to reframe them in a more positive light. For example, instead of focusing on what you don't have, focus on what you do have and express gratitude for it.

Volunteer or Give Back: Volunteering or helping others in need can help you appreciate what you have and feel grateful for the opportunity to make a difference in someone else's life.

Fostering a Positive Attitude:

In addition to practicing gratitude, fostering a positive attitude can help you achieve your goals and live a happier life. Here are some tips for cultivating a positive attitude:

10: HOW TO PRACTICE GRATITUDE AND FOSTER A POSITIVE ATTITUDE

Surround Yourself with Positive People: Surrounding yourself with people who inspire and motivate you can help you maintain a positive attitude.

Focus on Solutions, Not Problems: Instead of dwelling on problems, focus on finding solutions to overcome them.

Celebrate Small Wins: Celebrating small wins along the way can help you maintain a positive attitude and stay motivated.

Practice Self-Care: Taking care of yourself, both physically and mentally, can help you maintain a positive attitude and be more resilient in the face of challenges.

Maintain a Growth Mindset: Embrace the idea that you can always learn and grow, and that failures are opportunities to learn and improve.

Conclusion:

Practicing gratitude and fostering a positive attitude are powerful tools for transforming your mindset, achieving your goals, and living your best life. By incorporating these practices into your daily routine, you can cultivate a more

10: HOW TO PRACTICE GRATITUDE AND FOSTER A POSITIVE ATTITUDE

positive outlook on life and reap the numerous benefits that come with it.

11: Using Mindfulness to Cultivate Awareness and Stay Focused on Your Expectations

Introduction

Do you often find yourself distracted, unable to stay focused on your goals and expectations? Do you struggle to maintain a clear and centered mindset amidst the chaos of daily life? If so, you're not alone. Many people struggle with maintaining focus and awareness, which can make it difficult to achieve their goals and fulfill their expectations. In this chapter, we'll explore how mindfulness can help you cultivate awareness and stay focused on your expectations, allowing you to achieve the outcomes you desire.

What is Mindfulness?

Mindfulness is a mental state characterized by a heightened awareness of one's thoughts, feelings, and sensations, as well as the surrounding environment. It involves a non-judgmental acceptance of the present moment, as it is, without attachment to thoughts or emotions. Practicing mindfulness allows you to step back from your thoughts and feelings, observe them without judgment, and gain a deeper understanding of yourself and your experiences.

How Mindfulness Can Help You Achieve Your Expectations

Mindfulness can be a powerful tool for achieving your expectations. By cultivating awareness and staying focused on the present moment, you can gain greater clarity and insight into your goals and desires. This heightened awareness allows you to identify the actions and behaviors that will bring you closer to your expectations, and avoid those that will hold you back.

Additionally, practicing mindfulness can help you stay calm and centered amidst the stresses and distractions of daily life. This increased sense of calm can allow you to make more rational decisions, avoid impulsive behaviors, and stay focused on your goals and expectations.

Practical Techniques for Cultivating Mindfulness

There are many practical techniques you can use to cultivate mindfulness and stay focused on your expectations. Here are a few to get you started:

Mindful Breathing: One of the simplest and most effective

techniques for cultivating mindfulness is mindful breathing. Sit in a comfortable position, close your eyes, and focus your attention on your breath. Notice the sensation of the breath as it enters and leaves your body, and try to keep your mind focused on your breath. When your mind wanders, gently bring it back to your breath.

Body Scan: The body scan is a technique for bringing mindfulness to the physical sensations in your body. Lie down in a comfortable position and focus your attention on each part of your body, starting at your toes and working your way up to the top of your head. Notice any sensations in each part of your body, without judgment or attachment.

Mindful Walking: Mindful walking is a technique for bringing mindfulness to your movements. Take a walk outside, and focus your attention on each step you take. Notice the sensation of your feet as they touch the ground, the movement of your body as you walk, and the sights and sounds around you.

Mindful Eating: Mindful eating is a technique for bringing mindfulness to your food and the act of eating. Before you eat, take a moment to appreciate the appearance, aroma, and texture of your food. As you eat, focus your attention on the taste and sensation of each bite, and savor the experience.

Conclusion

Cultivating mindfulness is a powerful way to stay focused on your expectations and achieve your goals. By staying present in the moment and cultivating a sense of awareness, you can identify the actions and behaviors that will bring you closer to your desired outcomes. By incorporating mindfulness techniques into your daily routine, you can stay centered and focused, no matter what challenges come your way. So take a deep breath, focus your attention on the present moment, and start cultivating mindfulness today!

12: Overcoming Fear and Doubt: Tips for Maintaining Confidence and Overcoming Obstacles

Introduction:

Fear and doubt are natural emotions that everyone experiences at some point in their lives. They can hold us back from achieving our dreams and goals, and can leave us feeling stuck and helpless. However, it's important to recognize that fear and doubt are simply emotions, and they can be overcome with the right mindset and strategies. In this chapter, we'll explore tips and techniques for maintaining confidence and overcoming obstacles so that you can live your best life.

Recognize Your Fear and Doubt:

The first step to overcoming fear and doubt is to recognize that you're experiencing these emotions. Often, fear and doubt can manifest themselves as procrastination, avoidance, or even physical symptoms such as sweating or shaking. Once you recognize that you're experiencing fear and doubt, it's important to acknowledge these emotions and understand where they're coming from.

12: OVERCOMING FEAR AND DOUBT: TIPS FOR MAIN-TAINING CONFIDENCE AND OVERCOMING OBSTACLES

Reframe Your Thoughts:

One of the most effective ways to overcome fear and doubt is to reframe your thoughts. Instead of focusing on what could go wrong, try to focus on the positive outcomes that could result from your actions. For example, instead of thinking, "What if I fail?" try to think, "What if I succeed?" This shift in mindset can make a big difference in how you approach challenges.

Practice Self-Compassion:

It's easy to be hard on ourselves when we're experiencing fear and doubt. However, practicing self-compassion can help us to be kinder and more understanding towards ourselves. This means treating ourselves with the same kindness and care that we would give to a close friend or family member.

Visualize Success:

Visualization is a powerful tool for overcoming fear and doubt. When we visualize ourselves succeeding, we're more likely to feel confident and motivated to take action. Take a

12: OVERCOMING FEAR AND DOUBT: TIPS FOR MAINTAINING CONFIDENCE AND OVERCOMING OBSTACLES

few minutes each day to visualize yourself achieving your goals and experiencing the positive outcomes that come with success.

Take Action:

Finally, the best way to overcome fear and doubt is to take action. Often, we become more confident and less afraid when we take action towards our goals. Even small steps can help to build momentum and make us feel more capable of achieving our dreams.

Conclusion:

Fear and doubt can be challenging emotions to overcome, but with the right mindset and strategies, it's possible to maintain confidence and overcome obstacles. By recognizing your fear and doubt, reframing your thoughts, practicing self-compassion, visualizing success, and taking action, you can transform your mindset and achieve your goals. Remember, you have the power to create the future you desire – all you need is the courage to take the first step.

13: Developing a Growth Mindset: Embracing Challenges and Learning from Failure

Introduction:

The power of expectation lies in our ability to shape our beliefs, thoughts, and actions towards achieving our desired outcomes. However, it's not just about setting high expectations and hoping for the best. It's about developing a growth mindset that embraces challenges, learns from failures, and continuously strives to improve.

In this chapter, we will explore the concept of a growth mindset, its benefits, and practical strategies to cultivate it. We'll also look at how to overcome common obstacles and setbacks that can hinder our growth and success.

What is a Growth Mindset?

A growth mindset is the belief that our abilities and intelligence can be developed through dedication and hard work. It's the understanding that talent and intelligence are not fixed traits but can be improved through effort and persistence.

13: DEVELOPING A GROWTH MINDSET: EMBRACING CHALLENGES AND LEARNING FROM FAILURE

This mindset contrasts with a fixed mindset, where individuals believe that their abilities and intelligence are set in stone and cannot be changed. People with a fixed mindset tend to avoid challenges, give up easily, and view failure as evidence of their limitations.

On the other hand, people with a growth mindset embrace challenges, persist in the face of obstacles, and view failure as an opportunity for learning and growth.

Benefits of a Growth Mindset

Developing a growth mindset can have numerous benefits in different areas of our lives. Here are some of them:

Increased resilience: A growth mindset helps us bounce back from setbacks and failures by seeing them as opportunities for learning and growth.

Greater motivation: When we believe that our efforts and hard work can lead to improvement, we become more motivated to pursue our goals.

Improved performance: People with a growth mindset tend to perform better than those with a fixed mindset because they embrace challenges and persist in the face of obstacles.

More creativity: A growth mindset fosters creativity by encouraging experimentation, taking risks, and exploring new ideas.

Better relationships: A growth mindset helps us communicate more effectively, be open to feedback, and collaborate with others to achieve shared goals.

Strategies to Develop a Growth Mindset

Developing a growth mindset takes time and effort, but it's a skill that can be cultivated with practice. Here are some strategies to help you develop a growth mindset:

Embrace challenges: Instead of avoiding challenges, seek them out as opportunities to learn and grow. Challenge yourself to try new things, take on new projects, and step out of your comfort zone.

Learn from failure: Instead of viewing failure as a sign of weakness or incompetence, see it as a natural part of the learning process. Analyze your mistakes, identify what went wrong, and use that knowledge to improve your performance.

Practice persistence: Develop a "never give up" attitude and persist in the face of obstacles. When you encounter setbacks, remind yourself of your goals and keep moving forward.

Cultivate a love of learning: Develop a curiosity about the world and a passion for learning. Read books, take courses, and seek out new experiences that challenge your thinking and expand your horizons.

Adopt a growth mindset language: Pay attention to the words you use when describing your abilities and intelligence. Avoid using limiting language such as "I can't" or "I'm not good at this." Instead, use growth mindset language such as "I can improve with practice" or "I'm learning how to do this."

Obstacles to Developing a Growth Mindset

Despite the benefits of a growth mindset, there are many obstacles that can prevent us from developing it. Here are some common obstacles and strategies to overcome them:

13: DEVELOPING A GROWTH MINDSET: EMBRACING CHALLENGES AND LEARNING FROM FAILURE

Fear of failure: Fear of failure can paralyze us and prevent us from taking risks and trying new things. To overcome this fear, remind yourself that failure is a natural part of the learning process and an opportunity for growth.

Fixed mindset beliefs: If you have developed a fixed mindset, it may be challenging to change your beliefs. To overcome this obstacle, start by identifying the areas where you hold fixed beliefs and challenge them by seeking out evidence that contradicts them.

Negative self-talk: Negative self-talk can be a significant obstacle to developing a growth mindset. To overcome this, practice using positive affirmations and self-compassion when you make mistakes or encounter setbacks.

Lack of support: If you don't have a supportive environment or people in your life, it can be challenging to maintain a growth mindset. Seek out support from like-minded individuals, join a community or group that shares your values and beliefs.

Conclusion:

13: DEVELOPING A GROWTH MINDSET: EMBRACING CHALLENGES AND LEARNING FROM FAILURE

Developing a growth mindset is not an overnight process, but with consistent effort and practice, anyone can learn to embrace challenges, learn from failures, and continuously strive to improve. A growth mindset is a valuable skill that can help you achieve your goals, overcome obstacles, and live your best life. By adopting the strategies outlined in this chapter, you can cultivate a growth mindset that will serve you well in all areas of your life.

14: How to Manage Stress and Anxiety to Maintain a Positive Outlook

Stress and anxiety are two of the most common challenges that people face in their daily lives. They can come from various sources, such as work, relationships, health issues, or financial concerns. Regardless of the cause, the impact of stress and anxiety can be devastating, affecting our mental health, physical well-being, and overall quality of life.

The good news is that managing stress and anxiety is a learnable skill, and with the right tools and strategies, anyone can overcome these challenges and maintain a positive outlook on life. In this chapter, we will explore some practical tips and exercises that can help you manage stress and anxiety, transform your mindset, and live your best life.

Understanding Stress and Anxiety

Before we dive into the tips and exercises, it's essential to understand the nature of stress and anxiety. Stress is the body's natural response to perceived threats or challenges, such as a tight deadline, a difficult conversation, or a traumatic event. When we encounter stress, our body releases hormones, such as cortisol and adrenaline, to prepare us for fight or flight response.

Anxiety, on the other hand, is a prolonged and persistent feeling of worry, fear, or apprehension. It can arise from various sources, such as uncertainty about the future, social situations, or past traumatic experiences. Unlike stress, anxiety does not always have a clear trigger, and it can persist even when there is no immediate danger.

While stress and anxiety are different, they often go hand in hand, and the symptoms of one can exacerbate the other. For example, stress can trigger anxiety, and anxiety can cause physical symptoms, such as muscle tension, headaches, or digestive issues, which can increase stress levels. Therefore, it's crucial to learn how to manage both stress and anxiety to maintain a positive outlook on life.

Tips for Managing Stress and Anxiety

Here are some practical tips for managing stress and anxiety:

a) Identify the source of stress and anxiety

14: HOW TO MANAGE STRESS AND ANXIETY TO MAINTAIN A POSITIVE OUTLOOK

The first step in managing stress and anxiety is to identify the source of your distress. Take some time to reflect on what triggers your stress and anxiety and write them down. Once you identify the source, you can develop a plan to address them.

b) Practice relaxation techniques

Relaxation techniques, such as deep breathing, meditation, yoga, or progressive muscle relaxation, can help calm your mind and body and reduce stress and anxiety. Practice these techniques regularly, and you'll notice a significant improvement in your stress levels.

c) Exercise regularly

Exercise is an excellent way to relieve stress and anxiety. It releases endorphins, the body's natural feel-good chemicals, and helps reduce tension and fatigue. Aim for at least 30 minutes of moderate exercise, such as brisk walking, jogging, or cycling, most days of the week.

d) Get enough sleep

Sleep is crucial for mental and physical health. Lack of sleep can increase stress and anxiety levels, and make it harder to cope with daily challenges. Aim for 7-9 hours of sleep each night and practice good sleep hygiene, such as avoiding caffeine and electronics before bedtime.

e) Connect with others

Social support is vital for managing stress and anxiety. Connect with family, friends, or colleagues who can offer a listening ear, practical advice, or emotional support. Joining a support group or seeking professional counseling can also be helpful.

f) Practice self-care

Self-care is essential for maintaining mental and emotional well-being. Set aside time each day for activities that you enjoy, such as reading, listening to music, or taking a bath. Eat a balanced diet, stay hydrated, and avoid alcohol, tobacco, and drugs.

Exercises for Managing Stress and Anxiety

Here are some exercises that can help you manage stress and anxiety:

14: HOW TO MANAGE STRESS AND ANXIETY TO MAINTAIN A POSITIVE OUTLOOK

a) Gratitude journaling

Gratitude journaling is a powerful exercise that can help shift your mindset from negative to positive. Each day, write down three things that you are grateful for, no matter how small or big they may be. This exercise can help you focus on the good things in your life and increase your sense of well-being.

b) Visualization

Visualization is a technique that involves creating a mental image of a positive outcome or situation. Close your eyes, take a few deep breaths, and imagine yourself in a peaceful and relaxing place, such as a beach or a mountain. Visualize yourself feeling calm, happy, and confident. This exercise can help reduce anxiety and increase feelings of relaxation.

c) Mindful breathing

Mindful breathing is a simple yet effective exercise that can help you calm your mind and reduce stress and anxiety. Find a quiet and comfortable place to sit, close your eyes, and focus on your breath. Inhale deeply through your nose and exhale slowly through your mouth. Repeat this exercise for a few minutes, paying attention to your breath and letting go of any distracting thoughts.

d) Progressive muscle relaxation

Progressive muscle relaxation is a technique that involves tensing and relaxing different muscle groups in your body. Start by tensing your feet for a few seconds, then release the tension and feel the relaxation. Move on to your calves, thighs, stomach, chest, arms, and face, tensing and relaxing each muscle group for a few seconds. This exercise can help release physical tension and reduce stress levels.

e) Positive affirmations

Positive affirmations are short and powerful statements that you repeat to yourself to promote positive thinking and self-belief. Write down a few positive affirmations, such as "I am capable and confident," "I trust myself," or "I can handle any challenge that comes my way." Repeat these affirmations to yourself daily, either out loud or in your mind.

Conclusion

14: HOW TO MANAGE STRESS AND ANXIETY TO MAINTAIN A POSITIVE OUTLOOK

Managing stress and anxiety is an ongoing process that requires practice, patience, and perseverance. By incorporating these tips and exercises into your daily routine, you can learn to transform your mindset, overcome your challenges, and live your best life. Remember, you have the power to change your thoughts, beliefs, and attitudes, and unleash the power of expectation to create the future you desire.

15: The Importance of Taking Action: Moving Forward with Purpose and Intention

The power of expectation is an incredibly potent force in our lives, but it is not a magic bullet. Having a clear vision of what we want to achieve and an unwavering belief that we will achieve it is undoubtedly a crucial step in realizing our dreams, but it is only the beginning. If we want to make our expectations a reality, we must be willing to take action to bring them to fruition.

Taking action is a fundamental component of success, yet it is often the most challenging part of the process. Many of us get stuck in a cycle of analysis paralysis, endlessly contemplating our options without ever making a concrete decision or taking the first step. We may convince ourselves that we are waiting for the perfect opportunity, waiting for the stars to align, or waiting for some external factor to come into play that will make our path clear. But the truth is, there is no such thing as a perfect opportunity, and the stars will never align precisely as we want them to. We are the ones responsible for creating our own path.

15: THE IMPORTANCE OF TAKING ACTION: MOVING FORWARD WITH PURPOSE AND INTENTION

So how do we move forward with purpose and intention, even when the path ahead seems uncertain or intimidating? Here are some strategies to help you take action towards your goals.

Set Clear and Specific Goals

Before you can take action towards achieving your goals, you must first be clear on what those goals are. Setting clear, specific, and measurable goals helps to focus your efforts and keeps you on track. Break down your goals into smaller, manageable tasks, and set deadlines for each step along the way. This will help you to stay accountable and motivated, even when the going gets tough.

Develop a Plan of Action

Once you have identified your goals, develop a plan of action to achieve them. Break down your plan into smaller, manageable steps that you can take on a daily or weekly basis. Identify potential obstacles and develop contingency plans for dealing with them. Having a plan in place helps to keep you focused and gives you a roadmap for achieving your goals.

15: THE IMPORTANCE OF TAKING ACTION: MOVING FORWARD WITH PURPOSE AND INTENTION

Take Consistent Action

Consistency is key when it comes to taking action towards your goals. Set aside time each day or week to work towards your goals, and stick to that schedule as much as possible. Even small actions taken consistently over time can lead to significant progress.

Embrace Failure and Learn from Mistakes

Taking action towards your goals is not always smooth sailing. There will be times when you experience setbacks, obstacles, or failures. Embrace these challenges as opportunities to learn and grow. Reflect on what went wrong, identify what you can do differently next time, and use that knowledge to inform your future actions.

Surround Yourself with Support

Having a support system can be incredibly beneficial when it comes to taking action towards your goals. Surround yourself with people who believe in you and your vision, and who will encourage and motivate you to keep moving forward, even when things get tough.

15: THE IMPORTANCE OF TAKING ACTION: MOVING FORWARD WITH PURPOSE AND INTENTION

Practice Self-Care

Taking action towards your goals requires a significant amount of time, energy, and focus. It is essential to take care of yourself along the way. Incorporate self-care practices into your routine, such as exercise, meditation, or spending time in nature. Taking care of your physical, emotional, and mental health will help to keep you energized and motivated throughout the process.

In conclusion, taking action is a critical component of achieving our expectations. Setting clear and specific goals, developing a plan of action, taking consistent action, embracing failure, surrounding ourselves with support, and practicing self-care are all essential strategies for moving forward with purpose and intention. Remember that taking action requires courage, perseverance, and a willingness to step outside of our comfort zones. But the rewards of taking action towards our goals are immeasurable. By unleashing the power of expectation and taking intentional action, we can transform our lives and create the future we desire. Whether we are striving for personal growth, career success, or fulfilling relationships, taking action towards our goals is the key to unlocking our full potential and living our best lives.

One of the most important things to remember when taking action towards our goals is that progress, not perfection, should be our focus. It is easy to get bogged down in striving for perfection, but this mindset can be counterproductive. Instead, focus on making consistent progress towards your goals, even if that progress is slow or incremental. Celebrate your successes, no matter how small they may be, and use them as motivation to keep moving forward.

Another common obstacle to taking action towards our goals is fear. Fear of failure, fear of rejection, fear of the un-known - these are all natural fears that can hold us back from taking action. However, it is important to remember that fear is a natural part of the human experience, and it is something that we can learn to overcome. One way to do this is to reframe our perspective on fear. Rather than see-ing fear as a sign of weakness, see it as an opportunity for growth and learning. Embrace the discomfort of fear and use it as a tool for pushing yourself out of your comfort zone and towards your goals.

15: THE IMPORTANCE OF TAKING ACTION: MOVING FORWARD WITH PURPOSE AND INTENTION

Finally, it is important to recognize that taking action towards our goals is not a one-time event, but an ongoing process. Even after we have achieved our goals, there will always be new challenges and opportunities to pursue. The key is to maintain a growth mindset and a willingness to adapt and evolve as we continue to progress towards our vision of success.

In summary, taking intentional action towards our goals is a critical component of unleashing the power of expectation and transforming our lives. By setting clear and specific goals, developing a plan of action, taking consistent action, embracing failure, surrounding ourselves with support, practicing self-care, focusing on progress over perfection, overcoming fear, and maintaining a growth mindset, we can achieve our goals and create the future we desire. So go forth with purpose and intention, and take action towards your dreams today!

16: Creating a Vision Board: Using Visuals to Reinforce Your Expectations

One of the most powerful tools for reinforcing your expectations is creating a vision board. A vision board is a collection of images, words, and phrases that represent your goals and aspirations. It's a visual representation of the future you want to create for yourself.

A vision board serves as a reminder of what you want to achieve, and it helps you stay focused on your goals. It's a powerful tool for keeping your expectations high and reinforcing your belief that you can achieve anything you set your mind to.

In this chapter, we'll explore the process of creating a vision board and how it can help you unleash the power of your expectations.

Step 1: Define Your Goals

The first step in creating a vision board is defining your goals. What do you want to achieve? What are your aspirations? What would your ideal life look like?

16: CREATING A VISION BOARD: USING VISUALS TO REINFORCE YOUR EXPECTATIONS

Take some time to think about these questions and write down your answers. Be as specific as possible. The more specific you are, the easier it will be to find images and words that represent your goals.

For example, if your goal is to lose weight, you could be specific by setting a goal of losing 10 pounds in the next 3 months. Or if your goal is to start a business, you could be specific by setting a goal of launching your business within the next year.

Step 2: Collect Images and Words

The next step is to collect images and words that represent your goals. You can find images in magazines, online, or take your own photos. Look for images that resonate with you and represent your goals.

For example, if your goal is to lose weight, you could find images of healthy food, workout equipment, or people exercising. Or if your goal is to start a business, you could find images of entrepreneurs, office spaces, or products related to your business.

You can also find words and phrases that represent your goals. Write them down or cut them out of magazines. These words and phrases should be positive, inspiring, and reflective of your goals.

Step 3: Organize Your Vision Board

Once you have collected your images and words, it's time to organize your vision board. You can use a poster board or a bulletin board, or you can create a digital vision board using online tools.

Arrange your images and words on your board in a way that makes sense to you. You can organize them by theme or by goal. The important thing is to create a board that reflects your goals and inspires you to take action.

Step 4: Display Your Vision Board

Once you have created your vision board, it's important to display it somewhere where you will see it every day. This could be in your bedroom, your office, or any other place where you spend a lot of time.

Make sure your vision board is visible and that you take

time each day to look at it. Use your vision board as a reminder of your goals and aspirations. Let it inspire you to
take action and work towards your dreams.

Step 5: Take Action

Creating a vision board is just the first step in unleashing
the power of your expectations. The real magic happens
when you take action towards your goals.

Use your vision board as a roadmap for your life. Take action towards your goals each day, even if it's just a small
step. Celebrate your successes and learn from your failures.

Remember, your expectations are powerful. When you expect great things, you are more likely to achieve them. Your
vision board can help you stay focused on your goals and reinforce your belief in yourself.

Conclusion

Creating a vision board is a powerful tool for unleashing the
power of your expectations. It's a visual representation of
the future you want to create for yourself.

17: How to Set Realistic Expectations: Balancing Ambition with Practicality

Expectations are a powerful force that can shape the course of our lives. When we set our expectations high, we often achieve great things, but if our expectations are unrealistic or out of balance, they can lead to disappointment, frustration, and even depression. In this chapter, we'll explore how to set realistic expectations that balance ambition with practicality. We'll look at the benefits of setting realistic expectations, the risks of setting unrealistic expectations, and some practical strategies for finding the right balance.

The Benefits of Setting Realistic Expectations

Setting realistic expectations is essential for achieving our goals and living a fulfilling life. When our expectations are grounded in reality, we can make progress towards our goals and enjoy a sense of accomplishment along the way. Realistic expectations also help us avoid disappointment and frustration when things don't go as planned.

Another benefit of setting realistic expectations is that it allows us to stay motivated and focused. When we set goals that are too easy or too hard, we can lose motivation quickly. Goals that are too easy don't challenge us, and goals that are too hard can feel overwhelming. By setting realistic goals, we can stay motivated and focused on what we need to do to achieve them.

The Risks of Setting Unrealistic Expectations

On the other hand, setting unrealistic expectations can be a recipe for disaster. When our expectations are too high, we can quickly become discouraged, frustrated, and even depressed when we don't achieve them. Unrealistic expectations can also cause us to lose sight of what's really important and become obsessed with achieving our goals at all costs.

One of the most significant risks of setting unrealistic expectations is that it can lead to burnout. When we set goals that are too ambitious, we can push ourselves too hard, neglect our physical and emotional needs, and eventually burn out. Burnout can lead to a host of health problems, including chronic fatigue, depression, and anxiety.

Strategies for Setting Realistic Expectations

17: HOW TO SET REALISTIC EXPECTATIONS: BALANCING AMBITION WITH PRACTICALITY

So, how do we set realistic expectations that balance ambition with practicality? Here are some practical strategies:

Start with your why

Before you set any expectations, it's essential to understand why you want to achieve a particular goal. Understanding your why will help you set goals that are aligned with your values and priorities. It will also help you stay motivated when the going gets tough.

Break down your goals into smaller, manageable steps

One of the most effective ways to set realistic expectations is to break your goals down into smaller, manageable steps. This approach allows you to make progress towards your goal while avoiding overwhelm. It also helps you stay motivated by giving you a sense of accomplishment as you complete each step.

Be flexible and adaptable

When setting expectations, it's essential to be flexible and adaptable. Life is unpredictable, and things don't always go as planned. Being able to adapt to changing circumstances will help you stay on track towards your goals, even when unexpected challenges arise.

Use positive self-talk

Positive self-talk is a powerful tool for setting realistic expectations. When you use positive self-talk, you're reinforcing positive beliefs about yourself and your ability to achieve your goals. This can help you stay motivated and focused on your goals, even when things get tough.

Practice self-care

Finally, it's essential to practice self-care when setting expectations. Self-care includes things like getting enough sleep, eating a healthy diet, and taking time for relaxation and recreation. When you take care of yourself, you're better equipped to handle the challenges that come with pursuing your goals.

Conclusion

Setting realistic expectations is essential for achieving your goals and living a fulfilling life. When you balance ambition with practicality, you can make progress towards your goals while avoiding overwhelm and burnout. By using the strategies outlined in this chapter, you can set realistic expectations that are aligned with your values and priorities, stay motivated and focused on your goals, and maintain a healthy balance in your life.

Remember that setting realistic expectations doesn't mean settling for mediocrity or giving up on your dreams. Instead, it means being honest with yourself about what you can achieve and taking practical steps towards your goals. By setting realistic expectations, you're more likely to achieve your goals and enjoy the journey along the way.

In addition to the strategies outlined in this chapter, there are many other self-help resources and practical exercises that can help you set realistic expectations and achieve your goals. Some of these resources include books, podcasts, online courses, and coaching programs. Consider exploring these resources to find the ones that resonate with you and can help you achieve your goals.

Ultimately, setting realistic expectations is about finding the right balance between ambition and practicality. By being honest with yourself, breaking your goals down into manageable steps, staying flexible and adaptable, using positive self-talk, and practicing self-care, you can set realistic expectations that will help you achieve your goals and live your best life.

So, take some time to reflect on your goals and expectations. Are they realistic? Are they aligned with your values and priorities? Are you taking practical steps towards achieving them? By answering these questions honestly and taking practical steps towards your goals, you can unleash the power of expectation and create the future you desire.

18: Setting Boundaries and Prioritizing Self-Care to Support Your Expectations

Introduction:

In our fast-paced world, it's easy to get caught up in the hustle and bustle of everyday life. With so many responsibilities and obligations, it can be challenging to find time for ourselves. However, prioritizing self-care and setting boundaries is essential to achieving our goals and living the life we desire. In this chapter, we'll explore the importance of self-care and boundary setting, and how these practices can support our expectations and transform our mindset.

The Importance of Self-Care:

Self-care is a term that's become increasingly popular in recent years, and for good reason. It's essential for our physical, emotional, and mental well-being. Practicing self-care can help reduce stress, improve our mood, and increase our overall happiness. It's also an important aspect of achieving our goals and living the life we desire.

When we prioritize self-care, we're telling ourselves and

others that our needs matter. We're setting boundaries and saying no to things that don't serve us. We're also taking the time to nourish our minds, bodies, and spirits, which can help us feel more energized, focused, and motivated.

Some examples of self-care include getting enough sleep, eating healthy foods, exercising regularly, spending time in nature, practicing mindfulness or meditation, and engaging in hobbies or activities we enjoy. It's essential to find self-care practices that work for us and incorporate them into our daily routines.

Setting Boundaries:

Setting boundaries is another important aspect of prioritizing self-care and supporting our expectations. Boundaries are limits we set for ourselves and others to protect our well-being and prevent burnout. When we set boundaries, we're saying yes to things that serve us and no to things that don't.

Some examples of boundaries we can set include saying no to social events that don't interest us or will drain our energy, delegating tasks at work or home, and avoiding toxic relationships or situations. It's important to communicate our boundaries clearly and assertively, without feeling guilty or apologizing for them.

Setting boundaries can be challenging, especially if we're used to putting others' needs before our own. However, it's essential to remember that setting boundaries is not selfish; it's an act of self-love and self-respect. When we set boundaries, we're creating a healthy and supportive environment for ourselves, which can help us achieve our goals and live our best lives.

How Self-Care and Boundary Setting Can Support Our Expectations:

Practicing self-care and setting boundaries can support our expectations in several ways. Firstly, self-care can help us stay focused and motivated. When we take care of ourselves, we have more energy and mental clarity, which can help us tackle our goals with enthusiasm and determination.

Secondly, setting boundaries can help us avoid burnout and maintain a healthy work-life balance. When we set boundaries, we're prioritizing our needs and preventing ourselves from becoming overwhelmed or stressed. This can help us stay on track with our goals and avoid burnout or procrastination.

Finally, self-care and boundary setting can help us cultivate a positive mindset and outlook on life. When we prioritize our well-being and set boundaries that support us, we're telling ourselves that we're worthy and deserving of the life we desire. This can help us stay optimistic and motivated, even in the face of challenges or setbacks.

Practical Exercises to Support Self-Care and Boundary Setting:

If you're looking to prioritize self-care and set boundaries to support your expectations, there are several practical exercises you can try. These include:

Creating a self-care routine: Write down a list of self-care practices that nourish your mind, body, and spirit. Incorporate these practices into your daily routine, even if it's just for a few minutes each day.

18: SETTING BOUNDARIES AND PRIORITIZING SELF-CARE TO SUPPORT YOUR EXPECTATIONS

Identifying your values: Take some time to reflect on your values and what's important to you. Use this information to set boundaries and make decisions that align with your values.

Saying no: Practice saying no to things that don't serve you or align with your goals. Remember, saying no is not selfish; it's an act of self-love and self-respect.

Communicating your boundaries: Practice communicating your boundaries clearly and assertively. Use "I" statements to express your needs and avoid apologizing or feeling guilty for setting boundaries.

Setting realistic goals: Set goals that align with your values and prioritize your well-being. Avoid setting goals that are too challenging or overwhelming, as this can lead to burnout or procrastination.

Conclusion:

In conclusion, prioritizing self-care and setting boundaries is essential to achieving our goals and living the life we desire. By taking care of ourselves and setting limits that support us, we can stay focused, motivated, and optimistic, even in the face of challenges or setbacks. Remember, self-care and boundary setting are not selfish; they're essential practices that can help us unleash the power of expectation and transform our mindset. So, take some time today to prioritize your well-being, set some boundaries, and create the future you desire.

19: Navigating Negative Influences: Strategies for Staying Positive in a Negative World

Introduction:

In our world today, it's easy to feel overwhelmed by negativity. From news headlines to social media feeds, negativity can surround us at every turn. However, it's essential to remember that our thoughts and mindset have a significant impact on our lives. Navigating negative influences and staying positive is critical to achieving our goals and living our best lives. In this chapter, we'll explore strategies for staying positive in a negative world and transforming our mindset to unleash the power of expectation.

Understanding the Impact of Negative Influences:

Negative influences can have a significant impact on our lives, affecting our mood, motivation, and overall well-being. Exposure to negativity can cause us to feel anxious, stressed, and overwhelmed, making it difficult to stay focused on our goals and remain optimistic about the future.

Negative influences can come from a variety of sources, including news and media, social media, negative relationships, and even our own negative self-talk. It's essential to be aware of these influences and take steps to mitigate their impact on our lives.

Strategies for Staying Positive in a Negative World:

Limiting Exposure to Negative Influences: One of the most effective ways to stay positive in a negative world is to limit our exposure to negativity. This can include avoiding news and media that focus on negative events or limiting our time on social media.

Practicing Gratitude: Gratitude is a powerful tool for staying positive and shifting our mindset. Take some time each day to reflect on the things you're grateful for, whether it's a supportive friend, a beautiful sunset, or a delicious meal.

Focusing on Solutions: When faced with a negative situation, it's essential to focus on finding solutions rather than dwelling on the problem. By focusing on what we can do to make things better, we can maintain a positive outlook and feel empowered to take action.

19: NAVIGATING NEGATIVE INFLUENCES: STRATEGIES FOR STAYING POSITIVE IN A NEGATIVE WORLD

Surrounding Yourself with Positive People: The people we surround ourselves with can have a significant impact on our mindset. Surround yourself with positive, supportive people who inspire you and lift you up.

Engaging in Self-Care: Practicing self-care is critical to maintaining a positive mindset. Take some time each day to do something that nourishes your mind, body, and spirit, whether it's taking a walk in nature, practicing meditation, or indulging in a favorite hobby.

Challenging Negative Self-Talk: Negative self-talk can be a significant source of negativity in our lives. Challenge negative self-talk by replacing it with positive affirmations and self-talk that reinforces your strengths and abilities.

Cultivating a Growth Mindset: A growth mindset is the belief that our abilities and qualities can be developed and improved over time. Cultivate a growth mindset by embracing challenges, learning from failure, and focusing on progress rather than perfection.

Conclusion:

19: NAVIGATING NEGATIVE INFLUENCES: STRATEGIES FOR STAYING POSITIVE IN A NEGATIVE WORLD

In conclusion, navigating negative influences and staying positive in a negative world is critical to achieving our goals and living our best lives. By limiting exposure to negativity, practicing gratitude, focusing on solutions, surrounding ourselves with positive people, engaging in self-care, challenging negative self-talk, and cultivating a growth mindset, we can transform our mindset and unleash the power of expectation. Remember, our thoughts and mindset have a significant impact on our lives, so choose positivity and stay focused on the future you desire.

20: The Power of Community: Surrounding Yourself with Supportive People

The saying "no man is an island" is more than just a cliché. It's a fact that we all need a support system to thrive in life. This is why surrounding yourself with supportive people is crucial in achieving your goals and living your best life. In this chapter, we'll explore the power of community and how you can create a support system that will help you reach your full potential.

The Benefits of Community

Being part of a community offers numerous benefits. Here are some of them:

Support: Having people who understand and empathize with you is essential for your well-being. They provide you with emotional support during tough times and encourage you to keep going when you feel like giving up.

Accountability: A community can hold you accountable for your actions and help you stay on track towards your goals. When you know that other people are counting on you, it's easier to stay committed to your plans.

Networking: Being part of a community can help you expand your network and make new connections. You never know who you might meet that could help you in your career or personal life.

Learning: Communities are great places to learn from others. You can pick up new skills, gain knowledge, and get fresh perspectives on different topics.

Creating Your Support System

Now that you understand the benefits of community, it's time to create your own support system. Here are some steps you can take to get started:

Identify Your Needs: The first step is to identify what you need from a community. Do you want emotional support, accountability, networking opportunities, or a combination of these? Knowing what you want will help you find the right group of people to surround yourself with.

Find Your Tribe: Once you know what you're looking for, it's time to find your tribe. There are many ways to do this, including joining online groups, attending events, volunteering, or taking classes. Look for groups that align with your interests and values.

Be Open: When you join a new community, be open and willing to connect with others. Introduce yourself, share your story, and listen to others' stories. Building relationships takes time, but it's worth the effort.

Contribute: To get the most out of a community, you need to contribute. Share your knowledge and skills, offer support to others, and participate in group activities. The more you give, the more you'll get back in return.

Be Selective: Not all communities are created equal. You need to be selective about the groups you join and the people you surround yourself with. Make sure that the community you're part of is supportive, uplifting, and aligned with your values.

Maintaining Your Support System

Creating a support system is just the first step. You need to maintain and nurture it to reap the benefits fully. Here are some tips to help you do that:

Show Up: Consistency is key when it comes to building relationships. Show up regularly to group meetings and events, and be present when you're there. This will help you build trust and deepen your connections with others.

Communicate: Communication is essential in any relationship, including those in a community. Be open and honest about your feelings, needs, and goals. Ask for help when you need it and offer support to others when they need it.

Celebrate Successes: When someone in your community achieves a goal, celebrate it. This shows that you care and that you're invested in their success. It also helps create a positive, uplifting environment.

Be Respectful: Respect is crucial in any relationship. Treat others with kindness and consideration, even if you disagree with them. Remember that everyone has their own experiences and perspectives, and that's what makes a community diverse and valuable.

Manage Conflict: Conflict is inevitable in any group of

people, but it's essential to manage it effectively. Address issues openly and respectfully, and try to find a resolution that works for everyone. Remember that conflict can be an opportunity for growth and learning.

Evaluate Your Community: Periodically evaluate your community to ensure that it's still meeting your needs. If it's not, it may be time to look for a new group or make changes within your current community. It's essential to be honest with yourself about what's working and what's not.

The Power of Supportive People

Surrounding yourself with supportive people is one of the most powerful things you can do to achieve your goals and live your best life. When you have people in your corner, cheering you on and holding you accountable, you're more likely to succeed.

However, building a support system takes time and effort. You need to be willing to put yourself out there, connect with others, and contribute to the group. But the rewards are worth it. You'll have a network of people who understand you, support you, and help you grow.

20: THE POWER OF COMMUNITY: SURROUNDING YOURSELF WITH SUPPORTIVE PEOPLE

In conclusion, the power of community cannot be overstated. It's essential to surround yourself with supportive people who can help you achieve your goals and live your best life. By following the steps outlined in this chapter, you can create a support system that will help you thrive. Remember, the journey to success is not a solo one. You need a team to help you get there.

21: How to Embrace Change and Adapt Your Expectations to Life's Curveballs

Change is an inevitable part of life, and while it can be exciting, it can also be scary and overwhelming. Whether it's a new job, a move to a new city, or a relationship ending, change can disrupt our expectations and throw us off course. However, the ability to adapt to change and adjust our expectations accordingly is essential to living a fulfilling life.

In this chapter, we'll explore why change is necessary, how to embrace it, and practical strategies for adapting your expectations to life's curveballs.

Why Change is Necessary

Change is necessary because it allows us to grow and evolve as individuals. Without change, we would remain stagnant, and our lives would become boring and unfulfilling. Change is what allows us to discover new passions, explore new opportunities, and connect with different people.

Change can also be a catalyst for personal growth. When we

face new challenges, we are forced to push ourselves outside of our comfort zones and develop new skills. These experiences can help us build resilience, adaptability, and self-confidence.

Moreover, change is an inherent part of the natural world. Everything around us is in a constant state of flux, from the changing seasons to the shifting tides. Embracing change allows us to align ourselves with the natural rhythm of the universe and connect with the world around us.

How to Embrace Change

While change is necessary for personal growth, it can be challenging to embrace. Here are some tips for embracing change:

Recognize your emotions: Change can be accompanied by a range of emotions, from excitement to anxiety. Recognize these emotions and accept them without judgment. This will help you process your feelings and move forward.

Reframe your perspective: Instead of viewing change as a negative experience, reframe your perspective to see it as an opportunity for growth and learning. Look for the positive aspects of the situation and focus on the opportunities it presents.

Practice mindfulness: Mindfulness is the practice of being present in the moment without judgment. By practicing mindfulness, you can learn to accept change without getting caught up in negative thoughts or emotions.

Focus on the present: When facing a significant change, it's easy to get caught up in worries about the future. Instead, focus on the present moment and take things one step at a time.

Seek support: Change can be challenging, but you don't have to face it alone. Seek support from friends, family, or a therapist to help you navigate the transition.

Adapting Your Expectations

Once you've embraced change, it's essential to adapt your expectations to the new reality. Here are some strategies for doing so:

Set new goals: When facing a significant change, it's essential to set new goals that align with your new reality. For example, if you've moved to a new city, set goals for exploring your new surroundings, making new friends, and trying new experiences.

Re-evaluate your values: A significant change can also prompt you to re-evaluate your values and priorities. Take some time to reflect on what's truly important to you and adjust your expectations accordingly.

Be flexible: When adapting to change, it's essential to be flexible and open to new opportunities. Don't cling too tightly to your expectations, but instead, be open to the possibilities that come your way.

Embrace uncertainty: Change can be accompanied by uncertainty, but it's essential to embrace this uncertainty and trust in the process. Remember that change can be a catalyst for growth and learning.

Practice gratitude: Finally, it's essential to practice gratitude for the positive aspects of the change. This can help you maintain a positive mindset and stay motivated as you adapt to your new reality.

21: HOW TO EMBRACE CHANGE AND ADAPT YOUR EXPECTATIONS TO LIFE'S CURVEBALLS

Conclusion

Change is an inevitable part of life, and learning to embrace it is crucial for personal growth and fulfillment. By recognizing our emotions, reframing our perspective, practicing mindfulness, focusing on the present, and seeking support, we can learn to embrace change and adapt to new situations.

Adapting our expectations is equally important when facing change. Setting new goals, re-evaluating our values, being flexible, embracing uncertainty, and practicing gratitude are all strategies that can help us adjust our expectations and thrive in new situations.

Remember, change can be scary and overwhelming, but it can also be exciting and transformative. By embracing change and adapting our expectations, we can unleash the power of expectation and create the future we desire.

22: Recognizing and Celebrating Your Progress: Building Momentum and Motivation

When it comes to achieving our goals and creating the life we desire, there's one thing that's often overlooked: celebrating our progress. It's easy to get caught up in the pursuit of our goals and forget to take a step back and acknowledge how far we've come. But recognizing and celebrating our progress is essential for building momentum and motivation, and it's a powerful way to transform our mindset and achieve even greater success.

In this chapter, we'll explore the importance of recognizing and celebrating your progress, and we'll provide practical strategies and exercises to help you build momentum and motivation on your journey to success.

Why Celebrating Progress Matters

It's easy to get caught up in the day-to-day grind of pursuing our goals. We can become so focused on the finish line that we forget to appreciate the journey. But recognizing and celebrating our progress is essential for several reasons:

22: RECOGNIZING AND CELEBRATING YOUR PROGRESS: BUILDING MOMENTUM AND MOTIVATION

It boosts motivation: Celebrating progress is a powerful way to boost motivation. When we acknowledge our progress, we feel a sense of pride and accomplishment. This, in turn, fuels our motivation to keep going and achieve even more.

It builds momentum: Celebrating progress helps us build momentum. When we see that we're making progress, even if it's small, it gives us the momentum we need to keep moving forward.

It improves our mindset: Recognizing and celebrating our progress is a way to transform our mindset. When we focus on our progress, we shift our mindset from one of lack and scarcity to one of abundance and growth. This, in turn, helps us stay positive and optimistic, even when we face challenges and setbacks.

How to Recognize and Celebrate Your Progress

Now that we've established the importance of recognizing and celebrating progress, let's look at some practical strategies and exercises to help you do just that.

Keep a progress journal: Keeping a progress journal is an

excellent way to track your progress and celebrate your achievements. Start by writing down your goals and the steps you're taking to achieve them. Then, each day or week, take some time to reflect on what you've accomplished. Write down your successes, no matter how small they may seem. Seeing your progress written down on paper can be incredibly motivating and inspiring.

Celebrate small wins: Don't wait until you achieve a big goal to celebrate. Celebrate your small wins along the way. Did you make it to the gym three times this week? Did you have a productive day at work? Celebrate these accomplishments, no matter how small. Treat yourself to a favorite meal or activity, or simply take a moment to acknowledge your progress and give yourself a pat on the back.

Share your progress with others: Sharing your progress with others can be a great way to celebrate and build momentum. Share your achievements with friends, family, or a support group. Celebrate together, and let others cheer you on. You'll be surprised at how motivating it can be to share your progress with others.

Create a progress board: A progress board is a visual representation of your progress. Start by creating a board with your goals written on it. Then, as you make progress, add pictures, notes, or symbols that represent your achievements. Seeing your progress board each day can be incredibly motivating and inspiring.

Take time to reflect: Finally, take some time each week to reflect on your progress. Ask yourself what you've accomplished, what challenges you've faced, and what you've learned along the way. Reflecting on your progress can help you stay focused, motivated, and inspired.

Conclusion

Recognizing and celebrating your progress is essential for building momentum and motivation on your journey to success. By keeping a progress journal, celebrating small wins, sharing your progress with others, creating a progress board, and taking time to reflect, you'll transform your mindset and achieve even greater success. Remember, progress doesn't have to be huge to be worth celebrating. Every step forward, no matter how small, is progress, and every step forward is worth acknowledging and celebrating.

22: RECOGNIZING AND CELEBRATING YOUR PROGRESS: BUILDING MOMENTUM AND MOTIVATION

It's also important to remember that progress isn't always linear. There will be setbacks and challenges along the way, but that's okay. Recognizing and celebrating progress is a way to stay positive and optimistic, even when things don't go as planned. By celebrating your progress, you'll be able to stay motivated and focused on your goals, even when the going gets tough.

Finally, don't forget to celebrate the journey. Achieving our goals is important, but the journey is just as important. Celebrate the ups and downs, the twists and turns, and the lessons learned along the way. By embracing the journey and celebrating your progress, you'll create a mindset of growth and abundance, and you'll be able to achieve even greater success in all areas of your life.

In conclusion, recognizing and celebrating progress is a powerful way to build momentum and motivation on your journey to success. By keeping a progress journal, celebrating small wins, sharing your progress with others, creating a progress board, and taking time to reflect, you'll transform your mindset and achieve even greater success. So, take a moment to acknowledge your progress and celebrate your achievements. You've come a long way, and you deserve to celebrate your journey and all that you've accomplished so far.

23: Cultivating Creativity: Using Your Imagination to Create the Life You Want

We all have the power to create the life we want, but sometimes we get stuck in our own limited thinking. We limit ourselves by focusing on what we believe is possible and what we think we can achieve, rather than opening ourselves up to the infinite possibilities that exist in the universe. The truth is, we can achieve anything we set our minds to, as long as we believe in ourselves and our abilities.

One of the keys to unlocking our full potential is cultivating creativity. Creativity is not just about art, music, or writing; it's about using our imagination to come up with new and innovative solutions to problems, to see things from different perspectives, and to envision a future that is different from our present reality.

In this chapter, we will explore the power of creativity and how you can use your imagination to create the life you want. We will discuss the benefits of cultivating creativity, practical exercises to help you tap into your creative potential, and strategies for incorporating creativity into your daily life.

The Benefits of Cultivating Creativity

Cultivating creativity has many benefits. Not only does it help us come up with new ideas and solutions, but it also helps us to:

Reduce stress: Engaging in creative activities can be a great way to reduce stress and promote relaxation. When we are engaged in creative activities, we are focused on the present moment, which can help us to forget our worries and reduce anxiety.

Boost confidence: When we use our imagination to come up with new ideas and solutions, we feel a sense of accomplish-ment and confidence. This can help us to build our self-es-teem and believe in ourselves and our abilities.

Improve problem-solving skills: Creativity requires us to think outside the box and come up with new solutions to problems. This can help us to develop our problem-solving skills and find innovative solutions to challenges in our lives.

Increase productivity: Engaging in creative activities can help to increase our productivity by giving us a break from our routine and helping us to recharge our batteries. When we return to our work, we may have renewed energy and focus.

Enhance relationships: When we engage in creative activities with others, we can build stronger relationships and connect on a deeper level. This can help us to feel more connected and supported, which can be beneficial for our overall well-being.

Practical Exercises to Cultivate Creativity

There are many exercises you can do to cultivate your creativity. Here are a few practical exercises to get you started:

Brainstorming: Take a blank piece of paper and write down any ideas that come to mind. Don't worry about whether the ideas are good or bad, just write them down. Once you have a list of ideas, review them and see if there are any that you can use to solve a problem or achieve a goal.

23: CULTIVATING CREATIVITY: USING YOUR IMAGINATION TO CREATE THE LIFE YOU WANT

Mind Mapping: Draw a circle in the middle of a blank piece of paper and write your goal or problem inside the circle. Then, draw lines from the circle and write down any related ideas or solutions that come to mind. Continue to add ideas and solutions to the map until you have a comprehensive list.

Free Writing: Set a timer for 10-15 minutes and write anything that comes to mind. Don't worry about grammar, spelling, or punctuation, just write. This can help to clear your mind and tap into your creative potential.

Visualizing: Close your eyes and visualize yourself achieving your goal or solving your problem. Imagine every detail, including how you feel, what you see, and what you hear. This can help to stimulate your imagination and inspire new ideas.

Role-Playing: Pretend you are someone else, such as a famous inventor or a successful entrepreneur, and think about how they would approach your problem or goal. This can help you to think outside the box and come up with new solutions.

23: CULTIVATING CREATIVITY: USING YOUR IMAGINATION TO CREATE THE LIFE YOU WANT

Incorporating Creativity into Your Daily Life

Now that you have some practical exercises to cultivate your creativity, it's important to find ways to incorporate creativity into your daily life. Here are some strategies to help you do just that:

Make time for creativity: Set aside time each day or each week to engage in creative activities. This could be anything from painting to writing to cooking. Whatever it is, make it a priority and commit to doing it regularly.

Surround yourself with creativity: Surrounding yourself with creativity can inspire you and stimulate your imagination. Visit art galleries, attend concerts or plays, or read books by your favorite authors. Expose yourself to different forms of creativity to broaden your horizons.

Take risks: Creativity requires us to take risks and step outside our comfort zone. Don't be afraid to try new things and experiment with different approaches. Remember that failure is often a necessary step on the road to success.

Collaborate with others: Collaboration can be a powerful

tool for creativity. Work with others who share your interests and passions, and bounce ideas off each other. You may be surprised at the new perspectives and ideas that emerge from these collaborations.

Practice mindfulness: Mindfulness can help to quiet the mind and tap into our creativity. Take a few moments each day to practice mindfulness, whether it's through meditation, yoga, or simply taking a walk in nature. This can help to clear your mind and make space for new ideas to emerge.

Conclusion

Cultivating creativity is a powerful tool for transforming your mindset and creating the life you want. By tapping into your imagination and thinking outside the box, you can come up with innovative solutions to problems, achieve your goals, and live your best life. By incorporating practical exercises and strategies into your daily life, you can unleash the power of your imagination and unlock your full potential. Remember that creativity is not just for artists or writers, but for anyone who wants to live a more fulfilling and meaningful life.

24: How to Use Failure as a Stepping Stone to Success: Lessons from Famous Failures

Failure is a natural part of life. It's something that we all experience at some point in our lives. But what separates successful people from those who give up is their ability to use failure as a stepping stone to success. In this chapter, we will explore the stories of famous failures and how they used their failures to achieve success. We will also provide you with practical exercises to help you use failure as a catalyst for growth.

Walt Disney

Walt Disney was fired from his job at the Kansas City Star in 1919 because, according to his editor, he "lacked imagination and had no good ideas." He then went on to start his own company, Laugh-O-Gram Studio, which eventually went bankrupt. But instead of giving up, he moved to Hollywood and started creating cartoons featuring a character called Oswald the Lucky Rabbit. However, he lost the rights to the character and was forced to start from scratch. This led him to create Mickey Mouse, which was an instant success.

Lesson: Don't give up after a setback. Keep pushing forward and look for new opportunities.

Exercise: Write down three setbacks you've experienced in the past and how you overcame them. Then, write down three things you can do to overcome your current setback.

J.K. Rowling

J.K. Rowling was a single mother living on welfare when she wrote the first Harry Potter book. She was rejected by twelve publishers before finally getting a book deal. Even after getting a book deal, she faced many rejections from critics who claimed the book was too long and wouldn't sell. But she persisted and continued to write, eventually becoming one of the most successful authors of all time.

Lesson: Don't let rejection discourage you. Keep working on your craft and believe in yourself.

Exercise: Write down one thing you've been rejected for in the past and how you handled it. Then, write down three things you can do to improve your chances of success in the future.

Michael Jordan

Michael Jordan is widely considered one of the greatest basketball players of all time. But before he achieved success, he experienced many failures. He was cut from his high school basketball team, which motivated him to work even harder. He went on to play at the University of North Carolina, where he won a national championship. However, he faced more setbacks when he was drafted by the Chicago Bulls. The Bulls were a struggling team at the time, and Jordan was often criticized for being a ball hog. But he continued to work on his game and eventually led the Bulls to six NBA championships.

Lesson: Use setbacks as motivation to work harder and improve your skills.

Exercise: Write down one skill you want to improve and three things you can do to work on it.

Thomas Edison

Thomas Edison is one of the most famous inventors of all

time. But he experienced many failures before achieving success. He failed over 1,000 times while trying to create the light bulb. When asked about his failures, he famously said, "I have not failed. I've just found 1,000 ways that won't work." He eventually succeeded in creating the light bulb, as well as many other inventions that revolutionized the world.

Lesson: Embrace failure as a natural part of the learning process.

Exercise: Write down three things you've learned from past failures and how you can use those lessons to improve your future performance.

Conclusion

These are just a few examples of famous failures who used setbacks as opportunities to learn and grow. By changing your mindset and viewing failure as a stepping stone to success, you can achieve your goals and live your best life. Use the exercises provided to help you turn your failures into opportunities for growth and success. Remember, the only true failure is giving up.

25: The Importance of Persistence: Never Giving Up on Your Expectations

Introduction

Expectations are the fuel that drives our motivation and helps us stay focused on our goals. However, it is common for people to lose motivation when things don't go as planned or when they face obstacles along the way. The key to success is persistence, which means never giving up on your expectations, even when faced with challenges. In this chapter, we will explore the importance of persistence and how it can help you achieve your expectations.

What is Persistence?

Persistence is the ability to continue doing something, even when faced with challenges or obstacles. It is a vital trait to have if you want to achieve your expectations. It means that you have the determination and the willpower to keep going, even when the going gets tough. Persistence is not just about working harder; it's about working smarter and not giving up on your expectations.

25: THE IMPORTANCE OF PERSISTENCE: NEVER GIVING UP ON YOUR EXPECTATIONS

Why is Persistence Important?

Persistence is essential for several reasons. Firstly, it helps you develop a strong work ethic. When you are persistent, you are willing to put in the time and effort required to achieve your goals. You don't give up when things get hard; instead, you keep pushing forward. Secondly, persistence helps you build resilience. When you face challenges or setbacks, you learn from them and become stronger. Finally, persistence helps you develop a growth mindset. When you are persistent, you believe that you can improve and learn from your mistakes.

The Benefits of Persistence

There are several benefits to being persistent. Firstly, it helps you achieve your goals. When you are persistent, you don't give up on your expectations, and you keep working towards them. This means that you are more likely to achieve them in the end. Secondly, persistence helps you develop a positive attitude. When you are persistent, you believe that you can achieve your expectations, and you are more likely to have a positive outlook on life. Finally, persistence helps you develop self-discipline. When you are persistent, you are more likely to stick to your goals, even when faced with distractions or temptations.

How to Develop Persistence

Developing persistence takes time and effort, but it is possible. Here are some strategies you can use to develop persistence:

Set clear expectations

To be persistent, you need to have clear expectations. This means setting specific, measurable, achievable, relevant, and time-bound (SMART) goals. When you have clear expectations, you know what you are working towards, and you can measure your progress.

Focus on your why

Knowing your why is essential for developing persistence. Your why is your reason for wanting to achieve your expectations. It's the thing that motivates you when things get hard. When you focus on your why, you are more likely to stay persistent.

25: THE IMPORTANCE OF PERSISTENCE: NEVER GIVING UP ON YOUR EXPECTATIONS

Break your expectations down into manageable steps

Breaking your expectations down into manageable steps makes them feel more achievable. When you focus on small steps, you can make progress each day, which can be motivating.

Create a plan

Creating a plan helps you stay focused on your expectations. It means that you have a roadmap to follow, which can help you stay persistent. Your plan should include specific actions you need to take, deadlines, and resources you need.

Stay positive

Staying positive is essential for developing persistence. When you believe that you can achieve your expectations, you are more likely to stay persistent. Try to focus on the progress you are making, rather than the setbacks.

Keep learning

Learning from your mistakes is essential for developing persistence. When you face challenges or setbacks, try to learn from them. This can help you improve and become better equipped to handle similar situations in the future.

Conclusion

Persistence is the key to achieving your expectations. It is a vital trait to have if you want to succeed in life. By developing persistence, you can working towards your goals, even when faced with challenges and setbacks. Remember, persistence is not just about working harder, it's about working smarter and never giving up on your expectations.

Developing persistence takes time and effort, but it is worth it. By setting clear expectations, focusing on your why, breaking your expectations down into manageable steps, creating a plan, staying positive, and learning from your mistakes, you can develop persistence and achieve your expectations.

In addition to the benefits of achieving your expectations, being persistent can also have a positive impact on other areas of your life. It can help you develop a strong work ethic, build resilience, and develop a growth mindset.

25: THE IMPORTANCE OF PERSISTENCE: NEVER GIVING UP ON YOUR EXPECTATIONS

It's important to remember that developing persistence is a journey, not a destination. There will be times when you feel like giving up, but it's important to stay committed to your goals and keep pushing forward. When faced with challenges, remember that persistence is not about being perfect, it's about never giving up. Keep working towards your expectations, and you will achieve them in the end.

In conclusion, persistence is a vital trait to have if you want to achieve your expectations. By developing persistence, you can stay focused on your goals, even when faced with challenges and setbacks. Remember to set clear expectations, focus on your why, break your expectations down into manageable steps, create a plan, stay positive, and keep learning from your mistakes. With persistence, you can transform your mindset, achieve your goals, and live your best life.

26: Creating a Plan of Action: Breaking Down Your Goals into Manageable Steps

As you embark on your journey of unleashing the power of expectation, one crucial aspect that cannot be overlooked is creating a plan of action. Having a plan of action is essential because it helps you break down your goals into manageable steps, making them more achievable. In this chapter, we will explore the process of creating a plan of action and how to use it to transform your mindset, achieve your goals, and live your best life.

The first step in creating a plan of action is to identify your goals. It's important to set clear, specific, and measurable goals. This means breaking down your ultimate goal into smaller, more achievable objectives. For example, if your goal is to start your own business, your objectives could be to conduct market research, create a business plan, secure funding, and launch your business.

Once you have identified your goals, the next step is to prioritize them. It's important to focus on the most important goals first, as this will help you stay motivated and focused.

26: CREATING A PLAN OF ACTION: BREAKING DOWN YOUR GOALS INTO MANAGEABLE STEPS

You can prioritize your goals based on their importance, urgency, or difficulty level. For example, if your goal is to lose weight and also start your own business, you may want to prioritize losing weight first because it's more urgent for your health.

After prioritizing your goals, the next step is to create a timeline. This involves breaking down each objective into smaller, more manageable tasks and assigning a deadline to each task. For example, if your objective is to conduct market research for your business, you may need to break it down into tasks such as identifying your target market, researching your competitors, and analyzing consumer trends. You can then assign deadlines to each task to ensure you stay on track.

The next step in creating a plan of action is to identify the resources you will need to achieve your goals. This includes things like time, money, and support from others. For example, if your goal is to start your own business, you may need to allocate a certain amount of money for startup costs, and you may also need to seek advice and support from a mentor or business coach.

26: CREATING A PLAN OF ACTION: BREAKING DOWN YOUR GOALS INTO MANAGEABLE STEPS

Once you have identified your resources, the next step is to take action. This means executing your plan and taking the necessary steps to achieve your goals. It's important to stay committed and motivated, even when faced with challenges and setbacks. You may need to revise your plan of action as you go along, but always keep your ultimate goal in mind.

To ensure you stay on track, it's important to regularly review your plan of action. This means checking your progress against your timeline and making any necessary adjustments. It's also a good idea to celebrate your successes along the way, no matter how small they may seem. This will help keep you motivated and focused on your ultimate goal.

In addition to creating a plan of action, there are some other strategies you can use to help you achieve your goals. One such strategy is visualization. This involves imagining yourself achieving your goal and visualizing the steps you need to take to get there. You can also use affirmations, which are positive statements that reinforce your belief in yourself and your ability to achieve your goals.

Another strategy is to surround yourself with positive and

supportive people. This can include friends, family, mentors, or coaches. Having a support system can help you stay motivated and focused, and can also provide you with valuable advice and feedback.

In conclusion, creating a plan of action is essential to achieving your goals and unleashing the power of expectation. By identifying your goals, prioritizing them, creating a timeline, identifying your resources, and taking action, you can transform your mindset, achieve your goals, and live your best life. Remember to regularly review your plan of action, celebrate your successes, and use other strategies such as visualization and affirmations to stay motivated and focused.

27: How to Develop Self-Discipline and Stay Focused on Your Expectations

Developing self-discipline and staying focused on your expectations are crucial factors in achieving your goals and creating the future you desire. These skills require effort, commitment, and patience, but they can be developed through consistent practice and dedication. In this chapter, we'll explore various strategies and practical exercises that can help you develop self-discipline and stay focused on your expectations.

Understanding Self-Discipline

Self-discipline is the ability to control your thoughts, emotions, and behaviors in pursuit of a goal. It involves making conscious choices that support your long-term objectives, even when it's difficult or inconvenient to do so. Self-discipline is not a trait that some people are born with and others aren't; it's a skill that can be learned and strengthened with practice.

One of the key elements of self-discipline is delaying gratification. This means resisting the temptation to indulge in immediate pleasures that may distract you from your long-term goals. For example, if your goal is to save money for a down payment on a house, you may need to forego a fancy vacation or an expensive night out with friends. By delaying gratification and focusing on your long-term objectives, you're building your self-discipline muscles and increasing your chances of success.

Another important aspect of self-discipline is consistency. This means making a daily commitment to take small actions that support your goals. For example, if your goal is to write a book, you may commit to writing for 30 minutes every day, even if you don't feel like it. By making consistent progress towards your goal, you're building momentum and strengthening your self-discipline.

Strategies for Developing Self-Discipline

There are several strategies you can use to develop self-discipline and stay focused on your expectations. Here are some of the most effective ones:

Define your goals: It's hard to be self-disciplined if you don't have a clear idea of what you're working towards.

27: HOW TO DEVELOP SELF-DISCIPLINE AND STAY FOCUSED ON YOUR EXPECTATIONS

Take some time to define your goals and write them down. Be specific about what you want to achieve, and set realistic timelines for yourself.

Create a plan: Once you've defined your goals, create a plan for achieving them. Break down your goals into smaller, manageable steps, and create a timeline for completing each one. Having a clear plan will help you stay focused and motivated.

Practice mindfulness: Mindfulness is the practice of being present and fully engaged in the moment. It can help you develop self-discipline by increasing your awareness of your thoughts and emotions. When you're mindful, you're better able to recognize when you're tempted to stray from your goals, and you can make conscious choices to stay on track.

Build accountability: Having someone to hold you accountable can be a powerful motivator. Share your goals with a friend, family member, or coach, and ask them to check in with you regularly to see how you're progressing. Knowing that someone else is watching your progress can help you stay focused and committed.

27: HOW TO DEVELOP SELF-DISCIPLINE AND STAY FOCUSED ON YOUR EXPECTATIONS

Eliminate distractions: Distractions can be a major obstacle to self-discipline. Identify the things that tend to distract you from your goals, and take steps to eliminate or minimize them. For example, if social media is a major distraction, you may need to limit your use of it or delete the apps from your phone.

Practical Exercises for Developing Self-Discipline

In addition to these strategies, there are several practical exercises you can do to develop self-discipline and stay focused on your expectations. Here are some of the most effective ones:

Practice visualization: Visualization is the process of creating a mental image of your desired outcome. Take some time each day to visualize yourself achieving your goals. Imagine yourself taking the necessary steps, overcoming obstacles, and ultimately reaching your destination. Visualization can help you stay focused on your expectations and strengthen your self-discipline by reminding you of the bigger picture.

Use positive affirmations: Positive affirmations are statements that reinforce positive beliefs and attitudes. They can help you develop self-discipline by boosting your confidence and motivation. Choose a few affirmations that resonate with you, such as "I am capable of achieving my goals" or "I have the discipline to stay focused on my expectations," and repeat them to yourself regularly.

Set small goals: Setting small, achievable goals can help you build momentum and develop self-discipline. Choose one small goal that's related to your larger goal, and commit to achieving it within a specific timeframe. Once you've achieved that goal, set another one and continue building from there.

Practice self-care: Taking care of yourself physically, mentally, and emotionally can help you develop self-discipline by improving your overall well-being. Make time for exercise, healthy eating, rest, and relaxation. When you're feeling good, you're more likely to have the energy and motivation to stay focused on your expectations.

Embrace discomfort: Developing self-discipline often requires stepping outside of your comfort zone. Embrace discomfort by intentionally doing things that are challenging or uncomfortable. For example, if public speaking makes you nervous, sign up for a public speaking class or volunteer to give a presentation at work. By pushing yourself outside of your comfort zone, you're building your self-discipline muscles and becoming more resilient.

In conclusion, developing self-discipline and staying focused on your expectations are essential skills for achieving your goals and creating the future you desire. By using the strategies and practical exercises outlined in this chapter, you can strengthen your self-discipline and stay on track towards your goals. Remember, self-discipline is not a trait you're born with; it's a skill that can be learned and developed with practice. So commit to consistent effort and patience, and you'll be amazed at the progress you can make.

28: The Power of Accountability: Partnering with Someone to Help You Stay on Track

The journey to achieving our goals and living our best lives can be challenging and daunting at times. We may have a clear vision of what we want to achieve, but we often lack the motivation and discipline to take consistent action towards our goals. This is where the power of accountability comes in. Accountability is the act of being responsible for our actions and decisions. It means that we take ownership of our goals and commit to taking the necessary steps to achieve them. In this chapter, we will explore the power of accountability and how partnering with someone can help us stay on track and achieve our goals.

The Power of Accountability

Accountability is an essential component of success. When we are accountable, we take responsibility for our actions, and we are more likely to follow through on our commitments. Accountability provides us with the motivation and discipline we need to stay focused and consistent in our efforts. It helps us to overcome the obstacles and challenges that we face along the way.

Accountability also helps us to develop a growth mindset. A growth mindset is the belief that we can learn, grow, and improve. It is the opposite of a fixed mindset, which is the belief that our abilities and talents are predetermined, and we cannot change them. When we are accountable, we embrace a growth mindset because we recognize that we can improve and achieve our goals with effort and dedication.

Partnering with Someone

Partnering with someone is an effective way to increase our accountability. When we partner with someone, we have someone who can hold us accountable and provide us with support and encouragement. This person can be a friend, family member, or a coach. The key is to find someone who shares our vision and is committed to helping us achieve our goals.

When we partner with someone, we establish a sense of mutual accountability. We are accountable to ourselves, but we are also accountable to our partner. This creates a sense of obligation and responsibility, which can help us to stay on track and remain committed to our goals. It also provides us with a sense of community and connection, which can be essential for our mental and emotional well-being.

Practical Strategies for Accountability

There are many practical strategies we can use to increase our accountability. Here are some of the most effective strategies:

Set clear goals: Setting clear goals is the first step towards accountability. When we have clear goals, we know exactly what we want to achieve, and we can create a plan to get there.

Share our goals: Sharing our goals with our partner can increase our accountability. When we share our goals, we establish a sense of obligation and responsibility to follow through on them.

Create a plan: Creating a plan is essential for achieving our goals. We need to break down our goals into manageable steps and create a timeline for completing each step.

Schedule regular check-ins: Scheduling regular check-ins

28: THE POWER OF ACCOUNTABILITY: PARTNERING WITH SOMEONE TO HELP YOU STAY ON TRACK

with our partner can help us stay on track and ensure that we are making progress towards our goals.

Celebrate our successes: Celebrating our successes is an essential part of accountability. When we celebrate our successes, we reinforce our commitment to our goals and increase our motivation to continue.

Conclusion

In conclusion, accountability is an essential component of success. It helps us to stay focused, motivated, and disciplined in our efforts to achieve our goals. Partnering with someone is a powerful way to increase our accountability and ensure that we stay on track. By setting clear goals, creating a plan, scheduling regular check-ins, and celebrating our successes, we can unleash the power of accountability and transform our lives.

29: Building a Support System: Surrounding Yourself with People Who Believe in Your Expectations

Introduction

Expectations can be a powerful tool for creating the future you desire. But the journey to achieving those expectations can be a challenging one, full of obstacles, setbacks, and self-doubt. That's why it's crucial to have a support system in place that can help you stay motivated, focused, and on track.

In this chapter, we'll explore the importance of building a support system and surrounding yourself with people who believe in your expectations. We'll look at the different types of support you might need, from emotional to practical, and discuss how to find and cultivate the right relationships to help you reach your goals.

The Power of Support

Building a support system is a critical part of achieving your expectations. When you surround yourself with people who believe in you and your goals, you're more likely to stay motivated and focused. Support can come in many different forms, from emotional encouragement to practical help with specific tasks or challenges.

Having a support system can also help you stay accountable to yourself and your expectations. When you have people in your life who are invested in your success, you're more likely to stay committed to your goals and follow through on your plans.

Types of Support

Different types of support can be helpful at different stages of your journey toward achieving your expectations. Emotional support, for example, can be crucial during times of self-doubt or setbacks. Having people in your life who can provide encouragement, reassurance, and a listening ear can help you stay motivated and focused.

Practical support, on the other hand, can be invaluable when it comes to tackling specific challenges or tasks related to your expectations. This might include help with research, networking, or even just running errands or taking care of household tasks so you have more time and energy to focus on your goals.

Finally, professional support can also be important, particularly if you're pursuing a specific career or academic path. This might include mentors, coaches, or advisors who can provide guidance, feedback, and support as you work toward your goals.

Finding the Right Support

Building a support system starts with identifying the types of support you need and the people who can provide it. Here are some strategies for finding the right support:

Identify your needs: Take some time to reflect on the types of support you need to achieve your expectations. Do you need emotional support, practical help, or professional guidance? Are there specific challenges or obstacles you need help with?

Reach out to your network: Start by reaching out to the people in your existing network, such as friends, family, colleagues, or classmates. Let them know what you're working toward and the types of support you're looking for. You might be surprised by the number of people who are willing to help.

Join a community: Look for communities or groups that are focused on your area of interest or expertise. This might include online forums, local clubs or organizations, or even meetups or conferences. These communities can be a great way to connect with people who share your goals and interests.

Seek out professional support: If you're pursuing a specific career or academic path, look for mentors, coaches, or advisors who can provide guidance and support. This might include professors, industry professionals, or even online courses or coaching programs.

Cultivating Supportive Relationships

Once you've identified the types of support you need and the people who can provide it, it's important to cultivate those relationships in a way that's mutually beneficial. Here are some tips for building and maintaining supportive relationships:

Be clear about your expectations: Let the people in your support system know what you're working toward and what types of support you need. Be specific about your goals and how they can help.

Show gratitude: Make sure to express your appreciation and gratitude for the support you receive. This might include saying thank you, sending a thoughtful note or gift, or simply letting people know how much their support means to you.

Be available: Building supportive relationships is a two-way street. Make sure to be available and supportive to the people in your network as well. Offer to help with their goals and challenges, and be willing to listen and provide support when they need it.

Communicate regularly: Stay in touch with the people in your support system on a regular basis. This might include checking in via email, phone, or social media, or scheduling regular meetups or virtual hangouts.

29: BUILDING A SUPPORT SYSTEM: SURROUNDING YOURSELF WITH PEOPLE WHO BELIEVE IN YOUR EXPECTATIONS

Set boundaries: While it's important to be available and supportive to the people in your network, it's also important to set boundaries and prioritize your own needs and goals. Make sure to communicate your boundaries clearly and respectfully, and be willing to say no when necessary.

Conclusion

Building a support system is a crucial part of achieving your expectations. Whether you're pursuing a personal or professional goal, having people in your life who believe in you and your goals can make all the difference. By identifying the types of support you need, reaching out to your network, and cultivating supportive relationships, you can create a powerful support system that will help you stay motivated, focused, and on track as you work toward the future you desire.

30: Finding Inspiration: How to Stay Motivated and Inspired Throughout Your Journey

Introduction

In life, there are many challenges that we face, and it can be easy to become discouraged or lose our motivation. However, maintaining a positive mindset and staying inspired is essential to achieving our goals and living our best life. In this chapter, we will explore how to find inspiration and stay motivated throughout our journey.

The Importance of Inspiration

Inspiration is the fuel that drives us forward towards our goals. It is what keeps us motivated and focused when things get tough. When we are inspired, we are more likely to take action and pursue our dreams. Inspiration gives us the energy we need to push through obstacles and overcome challenges.

Without inspiration, we can easily become stuck in a rut, feeling unmotivated and unfulfilled. We may begin to doubt ourselves and our abilities, and we may give up on our goals altogether. That is why it is essential to find inspiration and keep it close to us throughout our journey.

Finding Inspiration

Inspiration can come from many sources, and it is different for everyone. Here are some ways to find inspiration:

Set goals and make a plan

Setting goals and making a plan is an excellent way to find inspiration. When we have a clear direction and know what we want to achieve, we are more likely to stay motivated and inspired. Write down your goals and make a plan to achieve them. Break your goals down into smaller, manage-able steps, and track your progress along the way. Celebrate your successes, and learn from your failures.

Surround yourself with positive people

The people we surround ourselves with can have a signific-ant impact on our motivation and inspiration. Surround yourself with positive, supportive people who believe in you and your goals. Avoid people who bring you down or dis-courage you. Seek out mentors and role models who can inspire and guide you.

Read books and listen to podcasts

Books and podcasts can be an excellent source of inspiration. Look for books and podcasts that align with your interests and goals. Read biographies of people who have
achieved great things and learn from their experiences.
Listen to podcasts that feature interviews with successful
people in your field or industry.

Explore new experiences

Exploring new experiences can be a great way to find inspiration. Try new things and step out of your comfort zone.
Travel to new places, try new hobbies, or attend conferences
and events in your industry. Experiencing new things can
help you see the world in a different way and inspire you to
pursue new goals.

Practice self-care

Practicing self-care is essential to finding inspiration. Take
care of your physical, emotional, and mental health. Exercise regularly, eat healthy foods, and get enough sleep.

30: FINDING INSPIRATION: HOW TO STAY MOTIV-ATED AND INSPIRED THROUGHOUT YOUR JOURNEY

Make time for activities that bring you joy and help you relax. When we feel good physically and emotionally, we are more likely to feel inspired and motivated.

Staying Inspired

Once you have found inspiration, it is essential to keep it close to you throughout your journey. Here are some ways to stay inspired:

Review your goals regularly

Reviewing your goals regularly can help you stay inspired. Keep your goals visible and review them daily. Celebrate your successes, and adjust your plan as needed. When you see progress towards your goals, it can be a great source of inspiration.

Celebrate your successes

Celebrating your successes is essential to staying inspired. Take time to acknowledge your accomplishments and celebrate your milestones. This will help you stay motivated and inspired to continue working towards your goals.

30: FINDING INSPIRATION: HOW TO STAY MOTIV-ATED AND INSPIRED THROUGHOUT YOUR JOURNEY

Keep learning

Continuing to learn and grow can be a great source of inspiration. Attend workshops, conferences, and seminars in your field or industry. Read books and articles that align with your interests and goals. When we are constantly learning, we are more likely to feel inspired and motivated.

Connect with others

Connecting with others can be a great way to stay inspired. Attend networking events, join groups or organizations related to your goals, and connect with like-minded individuals. Having a support system can help you stay motivated and inspired, as well as provide valuable insights and advice.

Practice gratitude

Practicing gratitude is a powerful way to stay inspired. Take time each day to reflect on the things you are grateful for in your life. Focus on the positive aspects of your journey and the progress you have made. When we focus on the good in our lives, we are more likely to feel inspired and motivated to continue working towards our goals.

Visualize your success

Visualizing your success can be a great source of inspiration. Imagine yourself achieving your goals and living your best life. Visualize the steps you need to take to get there, and imagine the feeling of accomplishment and fulfillment. When we visualize our success, we are more likely to feel inspired and motivated to work towards it.

Conclusion

Finding inspiration and staying motivated throughout our journey is essential to achieving our goals and living our best life. There are many ways to find inspiration, from setting goals and making a plan to practicing self-care and connecting with others. Once we have found inspiration, it is important to keep it close to us by reviewing our goals, celebrating our successes, and continuing to learn and grow. With these strategies, we can stay inspired and motivated to achieve our dreams and create the future we desire.

31: Overcoming Procrastination: Tips for Taking Action and Avoiding Distractions

Procrastination is a common challenge that many people face when trying to achieve their goals. It is the act of delaying or postponing tasks or actions, even when we know they are important. We often find ourselves procrastinating when we face tasks that seem overwhelming, uninteresting, or challenging. This can lead to frustration, stress, and a sense of unfulfillment. However, it is possible to overcome procrastination and take action towards our goals. In this chapter, we will explore practical tips and strategies that can help you overcome procrastination and achieve your goals.

Understand the root cause of procrastination

The first step in overcoming procrastination is to understand the root cause of the behavior. There are several reasons why people procrastinate, including fear of failure, perfectionism, lack of motivation, and lack of clarity. Once you identify the underlying cause of your procrastination, you can begin to develop strategies to address it.

31: OVERCOMING PROCRASTINATION: TIPS FOR TAKING ACTION AND AVOIDING DISTRACTIONS

Develop a plan

One effective way to overcome procrastination is to develop a plan. This plan should include a clear set of goals, deadlines, and a detailed action plan. By breaking down your goals into smaller, more manageable tasks, you can make progress towards your goals, even when faced with obstacles or distractions. It is also important to set realistic deadlines and hold yourself accountable for completing each task on time.

Eliminate distractions

Distractions are a common reason why people procrastinate. To overcome this, you need to identify the distractions that are most likely to interfere with your work and find ways to eliminate or minimize them. This may involve turning off your phone, closing your email, or finding a quiet space to work. If you find yourself easily distracted by social media or other online activities, you can use tools such as website blockers or apps that limit your access to these distractions.

Take small steps

31: OVERCOMING PROCRASTINATION: TIPS FOR TAKING ACTION AND AVOIDING DISTRACTIONS

When faced with a daunting task, it is easy to become overwhelmed and procrastinate. To overcome this, it is important to break down the task into smaller, more manageable steps. By taking small steps towards your goal, you can build momentum and confidence, which can help you overcome procrastination and stay motivated.

Celebrate progress

Celebrating progress is an important part of overcoming procrastination. When you achieve a small goal or complete a task, take time to acknowledge your progress and celebrate your success. This can help you stay motivated and focused on your goals.

Use positive self-talk

Positive self-talk is an effective way to overcome procrastination. When you find yourself procrastinating, use positive affirmations to motivate yourself. For example, you can tell yourself, "I am capable of completing this task" or "I am making progress towards my goal." By using positive self-talk, you can overcome negative thoughts and beliefs that may be holding you back.

31: OVERCOMING PROCRASTINATION: TIPS FOR TAKING ACTION AND AVOIDING DISTRACTIONS

Set priorities

Setting priorities is an important part of overcoming procrastination. By prioritizing your tasks, you can focus on the most important tasks and avoid procrastinating on less important tasks. It is also important to schedule your tasks based on your energy levels and productivity. For example, if you are most productive in the morning, schedule your most important tasks for the morning.

Find an accountability partner

Having an accountability partner is a powerful way to overcome procrastination. This can be a friend, family member, or colleague who can hold you accountable for completing your tasks on time. By sharing your goals and progress with someone else, you can stay motivated and focused on your goals.

Practice self-care

Self-care is an important part of overcoming procrastination. When we neglect our physical and mental health, we can become overwhelmed and lose motivation. To overcome procrastination, it is important to practice self-care by getting enough sleep, eating healthy, and exercising regularly. By taking care of your physical and mental health, you can stay motivated and focused on your goals, and have the energy and clarity of mind to take action towards achieving them.

Visualize success

Visualizing success is a powerful tool for overcoming procrastination. Take some time to visualize yourself successfully completing your tasks and achieving your goals. Imagine how it would feel to accomplish your goals, and the sense of satisfaction and fulfillment you would experience. By visualizing success, you can stay motivated and focused on your goals, even when faced with challenges or obstacles.

Reward yourself

Rewarding yourself for completing tasks is a great way to overcome procrastination. When you complete a task or reach a milestone, give yourself a reward. This can be as simple as taking a break, treating yourself to your favorite food or activity, or doing something that makes you happy.

31: OVERCOMING PROCRASTINATION: TIPS FOR TAK-ING ACTION AND AVOIDING DISTRACTIONS

By rewarding yourself, you can stay motivated and focused on your goals.

Final Thoughts

Procrastination can be a major obstacle to achieving our goals and living our best life. However, by understanding the root cause of procrastination and implementing practical tips and strategies, we can overcome this challenge and take action towards our goals. Remember to develop a plan, eliminate distractions, take small steps, celebrate progress, use positive self-talk, set priorities, find an accountability partner, practice self-care, visualize success, and reward yourself. By implementing these strategies, you can unleash the power of expectation and transform your mindset to achieve your goals and live your best life.

32: Staying Committed to Your Expectations: How to Stay on Track When the Going Gets Tough

When we first set our expectations and goals, we are often filled with excitement and motivation. We can envision ourselves achieving success and creating the future we desire. However, as time passes, we may find that staying committed to our expectations becomes increasingly difficult. We may encounter setbacks and obstacles that make us feel discouraged, frustrated, and overwhelmed. In this chapter, we will explore strategies for staying committed to your expectations and achieving your goals even when the going gets tough.

Understand Your Why

One of the most important steps in staying committed to your expectations is understanding your why. Why do you want to achieve your goals? What is the deeper motivation behind your expectations? When we understand our why, we are better able to stay committed and motivated, even when we encounter obstacles.

To understand your why, take some time to reflect on your

expectations and goals. Ask yourself why you want to achieve them. What will achieving these goals allow you to do? What impact will it have on your life? Write down your answers and refer to them regularly to stay focused and motivated.

Set Realistic Expectations

Another important factor in staying committed to your expectations is setting realistic goals. When we set expectations that are too high or unrealistic, we may become overwhelmed and lose motivation when we fail to achieve them. To avoid this, it's important to set goals that are challenging but achievable.

To set realistic expectations, break down your larger goals into smaller, more manageable steps. This will help you to see progress and stay motivated. Set deadlines for each step and hold yourself accountable to them.

Celebrate Small Wins

Celebrating small wins along the way is an important part of staying committed to your expectations. When we achieve small goals or milestones, it helps us to stay motivated and focused on our larger goals.

To celebrate small wins, set up a reward system for yourself. For example, if you complete a certain task or achieve a small goal, reward yourself with something you enjoy, such as a movie night or a special treat.

Surround Yourself with Supportive People

Surrounding yourself with supportive people can also help you to stay committed to your expectations. When we have a support system in place, we are better able to stay motivated and push through difficult times.

To surround yourself with supportive people, seek out friends and family members who encourage and support your goals. Joining a community or group of like-minded individuals can also provide valuable support and motivation.

Stay Flexible and Adapt

Staying committed to your expectations also requires flexibility and the ability to adapt. Setbacks and obstacles are inevitable, and it's important to be able to adjust your expectations and goals as needed.

To stay flexible and adapt, regularly assess your progress and make adjustments as needed. If you encounter an obstacle or setback, evaluate your approach and consider new strategies for moving forward.

Practice Self-Care

Finally, practicing self-care is an important part of staying committed to your expectations. When we take care of ourselves physically, mentally, and emotionally, we are better able to stay motivated and focused on our goals.

To practice self-care, prioritize activities that help you to feel relaxed and rejuvenated. This might include exercise, meditation, spending time in nature, or practicing a hobby you enjoy.

In conclusion, staying committed to your expectations requires a combination of strategies, including understanding your why, setting realistic goals, celebrating small wins, surrounding yourself with supportive people, staying flexible and adapting, and practicing self-care. By incorporating these strategies into your daily life, you can stay on track and achieve the goals you've set for yourself. Remember, success is not just about achieving your goals, but about the journey you take to get there.

33: The Importance of Patience: Understanding that Change Takes Time

Patience is a virtue, and it is one that can help you achieve your goals and live your best life. When it comes to creating the future you desire, patience is a critical component of success. In this chapter, we will explore the importance of patience in achieving your goals and how you can cultivate this essential skill.

Many of us live in a world where we expect everything to be instant. We want instant gratification, instant results, and instant success. However, the truth is that change takes time. When we try to rush the process, we can become frustrated, stressed, and even give up entirely. The key to achieving your goals is to understand that change takes time, and that success is a journey, not a destination.

It's important to have a long-term perspective when it comes to your goals. The reality is that most significant achievements take years, if not decades, to accomplish. For example, becoming a doctor, building a successful business, or writing a book all require patience, hard work, and perseverance. While these goals may seem daunting, remember that they are attainable with the right mindset and approach.

One of the most significant benefits of patience is that it can help you develop resilience. Resilience is the ability to bounce back from setbacks, and it is a crucial trait for achieving success. When you have patience, you can weather the ups and downs that come with pursuing your goals. You can stay focused on your long-term vision and keep moving forward, even when things get tough.

Another benefit of patience is that it can help you stay grounded in the present moment. When you are always focused on the future, you can become anxious and stressed about the unknown. However, when you have patience, you can enjoy the journey and appreciate the progress you are making. You can be present in the moment and savor each step along the way.

To cultivate patience, it's important to develop a growth mindset. A growth mindset is the belief that you can improve your abilities and develop new skills over time. When you have a growth mindset, you are more willing to embrace challenges and setbacks as opportunities for growth. You are less likely to give up when things get tough and more likely to keep pushing forward.

One way to develop a growth mindset is to practice self-compassion. Self-compassion is the practice of treating yourself with kindness, understanding, and forgiveness. When you make mistakes or experience setbacks, instead of beating yourself up, try to be kind to yourself. Recognize that you are doing your best, and that mistakes and setbacks are a natural part of the learning process.

Another way to cultivate patience is to set realistic goals. When you set goals that are too lofty or unrealistic, you are setting yourself up for failure. Instead, set goals that are challenging but achievable. Break down your goals into smaller, more manageable steps, and celebrate each accomplishment along the way. By setting realistic goals, you can build momentum and stay motivated as you work towards your long-term vision.

Finally, it's important to surround yourself with people who support and encourage your goals. When you have a strong support system, you can draw on their encouragement and inspiration when you need it most. Surround yourself with people who believe in you and your vision, and who are willing to support you through the ups and downs of the journey.

In conclusion, patience is a critical component of success. When you have patience, you can develop resilience, stay grounded in the present moment, and cultivate a growth mindset. To cultivate patience, develop a growth mindset, practice self-compassion, set realistic goals, and surround yourself with a strong support system. Remember that change takes time, and that success is a journey, not a destination. With patience, perseverance, and the right mindset, you can achieve your goals and create the future you desire. It's essential to remember that success doesn't happen overnight, and there are often setbacks along the way. However, with patience, you can weather the storms and keep moving forward.

It's also important to acknowledge that patience is not always easy. It's easy to become frustrated or lose motivation when progress feels slow. However, it's crucial to recognize that progress doesn't always happen in a straight line. There

will be ups and downs, but the key is to keep pushing forward, even when things get tough.

One way to stay motivated during times of frustration is to
reflect on how far you've come. Celebrate your accomplishments and remind yourself of the progress you've made. It's
easy to get caught up in the future and forget about the progress you've already made. However, reflecting on your progress can help you stay motivated and remind you of why
you started in the first place.

Another way to cultivate patience is to focus on the process
rather than the outcome. When you focus solely on the outcome, you can become fixated on the end result and lose
sight of the journey. However, when you focus on the process, you can enjoy the small victories along the way and appreciate the progress you're making.

It's also important to practice mindfulness to cultivate patience. Mindfulness is the practice of being present in the
moment and paying attention to your thoughts and feelings
without judgment. When you practice mindfulness, you can
become more aware of your thoughts and emotions and
learn to manage them more effectively. This can help you

stay grounded and patient as you work towards your goals.

Finally, it's important to recognize that patience is a skill that can be developed over time. It's not something that comes naturally to everyone, and that's okay. By practicing patience regularly and making a conscious effort to cultivate this skill, you can become more patient and resilient over time.

In summary, patience is a critical component of success, and it's a skill that can be developed over time. To cultivate patience, focus on the process rather than the outcome, reflect on your progress, practice mindfulness, and surround yourself with a strong support system. Remember that change takes time, and success is a journey, not a destination. With patience, perseverance, and the right mindset, you can achieve your goals and create the future you desire.

34: The Power of Forgiveness: Letting Go of Past Mistakes and Moving Forward with Expectation

The power of forgiveness is often underestimated. We have all been hurt at some point in our lives, whether it be a betrayal, a broken heart, or a lost opportunity. Holding onto past hurts can be detrimental to our emotional, mental, and even physical health. But what is forgiveness, and how can we harness its power to transform our lives and create the future we desire?

Forgiveness is a conscious decision to let go of anger, resentment, and bitterness towards someone who has wronged us. It does not mean that we condone or excuse their behavior, but rather that we choose to release ourselves from the negative emotions that are holding us back. Forgiveness is not an easy process, but it is essential for our well-being and personal growth.

One of the main benefits of forgiveness is that it allows us to move forward with our lives. When we hold onto anger and resentment, we are stuck in the past, unable to fully embrace the present or look towards the future. Forgiveness frees us from this emotional baggage, enabling us to live in the present and create the future we desire.

Moreover, forgiveness has been linked to numerous health benefits, both mental and physical. Studies have shown that forgiving others can lead to lower levels of stress, anxiety, and depression, as well as improved immune function and cardiovascular health. By releasing negative emotions, we can also experience greater happiness, optimism, and overall life satisfaction.

But how can we cultivate forgiveness in our lives? Here are some practical strategies and exercises to help you let go of past hurts and move forward with expectation.

Acknowledge Your Pain

The first step in forgiveness is acknowledging the pain that someone has caused you. This can be a difficult and emotional process, but it is essential for healing. Take some time to reflect on your feelings, write them down in a journal, or talk to a trusted friend or therapist. Recognize that it is okay to feel hurt, angry, or disappointed, and allow yourself to experience these emotions.

Practice Empathy

Empathy is the ability to understand and share the feelings of another person. By practicing empathy towards those who have hurt us, we can begin to see things from their perspective and understand their motivations. This does not mean that we condone their behavior or excuse their actions, but it can help us to let go of resentment and anger.

Let Go of Blame

Blame is often a defense mechanism that we use to protect ourselves from our own feelings of guilt or shame. However, blaming others only perpetuates negative emotions and does not lead to healing or growth. Instead, take responsibility for your own emotions and actions, and recognize that forgiveness is ultimately for your own benefit.

Choose to Forgive

Forgiveness is a choice that we make, and it is not always an easy one. However, it is a decision that can lead to profound transformation and growth. Choose to forgive others, even if you do not feel ready or willing to do so. This decision can be a powerful catalyst for healing and growth.

Practice Gratitude

Gratitude is the practice of focusing on the positive aspects of our lives, even in the face of adversity. By cultivating gratitude, we can shift our perspective from one of negativity and bitterness to one of positivity and abundance. Take some time each day to reflect on the things that you are grateful for, and focus on the positive aspects of your life.

Use Affirmations

Affirmations are positive statements that we repeat to ourselves, often in the form of a mantra or visualization. By using affirmations, we can reprogram our subconscious mind to focus on positivity and expectation. Create a list of positive affirmations that resonate with you, and repeat them daily to reinforce your commitment to forgiveness and growth.

Practice Self-Care

34: THE POWER OF FORGIVENESS: LETTING GO OF PAST MISTAKES AND MOVING FORWARD WITH EXPECTATION

Self-care is essential for our well-being and personal growth, especially when we are dealing with difficult emotions like anger and resentment. Take care of yourself by practicing healthy habits like exercise, healthy eating, and getting enough sleep. Engage in activities that bring you joy and fulfillment, such as hobbies, socializing with friends, or spending time in nature.

Seek Support

Forgiveness can be a difficult and emotional process, and it is okay to seek support from others. Talk to a trusted friend, family member, or therapist about your feelings and struggles. Join a support group or seek out resources online to connect with others who are going through similar experiences. Remember, you are not alone in your journey towards forgiveness and healing.

In conclusion, forgiveness is a powerful tool that can transform our lives and enable us to create the future we desire. By letting go of past hurts, we can release ourselves from negative emotions and move forward with positivity and expectation. Use the strategies and exercises outlined in this

34: THE POWER OF FORGIVENESS: LETTING GO OF PAST MISTAKES AND MOVING FORWARD WITH EX-PECTATION

chapter to cultivate forgiveness in your life, and experience the profound benefits of letting go and moving forward.

35: How to Give Back and Use Your Expectations to Help Others

Introduction:

Expectation is a powerful force that can help you achieve your goals, but it's not just about personal success. It's also about giving back to others and using your expectations to help them achieve their dreams. In this chapter, we'll explore the ways in which you can give back and use your expectations to help others.

Section 1: Understanding the Power of Giving Back

Giving back is a powerful way to use your expectations to help others. When you give back, you're not just making a positive impact on someone else's life, but you're also making a positive impact on your own life. Giving back can help you build relationships, develop new skills, and gain a sense of purpose and fulfillment.

There are many ways to give back, from volunteering your time to donating money to a worthy cause. One effective way to give back is to use your expertise and knowledge to help others. For example, if you're an expert in a certain field, you can volunteer to mentor someone who is just starting out. This can help them learn from your experience and accelerate their growth.

Section 2: Using Your Expectations to Help Others

Your expectations can also be a powerful tool for helping others. When you have high expectations for someone, you're essentially telling them that you believe in them and that you see their potential. This can be incredibly motivating and inspiring, and it can help them achieve things they never thought possible.

There are several ways to use your expectations to help others. One effective way is to set high expectations for someone and then hold them accountable. For example, if you're a coach or a mentor, you can set challenging goals for your clients or mentees and then hold them accountable for achieving those goals. This can help them develop a growth mindset and build confidence in their abilities.

Another way to use your expectations to help others is to provide positive feedback and encouragement. When someone is doing well, it's important to acknowledge their progress and offer words of encouragement. This can help them stay motivated and continue to strive for excellence.

Section 3: Practical Exercises for Giving Back and Using Your Expectations to Help Others

There are several practical exercises that you can use to give back and use your expectations to help others. Here are a few examples:

Volunteer your time: Find a local charity or nonprofit organization that aligns with your values and interests, and volunteer your time. This can be a great way to make a positive impact on your community and meet new people.

Mentor someone: Offer to mentor someone who is just starting out in your field. Share your experience and knowledge with them, and help them develop the skills they need to succeed.

Set challenging goals: Set challenging goals for someone and then hold them accountable for achieving those goals. This can help them develop a growth mindset and build confidence in their abilities.

35: HOW TO GIVE BACK AND USE YOUR EXPECTATIONS TO HELP OTHERS

Provide positive feedback: When someone is doing well, provide positive feedback and encouragement. This can help them stay motivated and continue to strive for excellence.

Conclusion:

Giving back and using your expectations to help others can be incredibly rewarding. Not only does it help you make a positive impact on someone else's life, but it also helps you develop new skills, build relationships, and gain a sense of purpose and fulfillment. So, whether you're volunteering your time or using your expertise to mentor someone, remember that you have the power to make a difference in the lives of others.

36: Conclusion: Living Your Best Life with the Power of Expectation

As we come to the end of this journey, it's important to reflect on everything we've learned about the power of expectation. We've explored the science behind how expectations can shape our thoughts, emotions, and behaviors, and we've looked at practical ways to use the power of expectation to transform our lives.

Expectation is a powerful force that can propel us towards our goals, or hold us back from achieving our full potential. When we have positive expectations, we are more likely to approach challenges with confidence, take risks, and persevere in the face of setbacks. On the other hand, negative expectations can lead to self-doubt, fear, and a sense of defeat before we even begin.

One of the most important things we've learned is that our expectations are not set in stone. We have the power to shape our expectations and beliefs, and therefore, the outcomes we experience in our lives. By using positive affirmations, visualization techniques, and mindfulness practices, we can reprogram our minds to expect success and abundance in all areas of our lives.

36: CONCLUSION: LIVING YOUR BEST LIFE WITH THE POWER OF EXPECTATION

But it's not just about changing our thoughts. We also need to take action to support our positive expectations. This means setting clear goals, creating a plan of action, and taking consistent steps towards our desired outcomes. When we combine positive expectations with intentional action, we create a powerful momentum that propels us towards success.

Of course, none of this is easy. Changing our expectations and taking intentional action requires dedication, patience, and a willingness to confront our fears and limiting beliefs. But it's worth it. When we live with the power of expectation, we unlock our full potential and create a life that is truly fulfilling and joyful.

So, as you move forward on your journey, I encourage you to continue to cultivate the power of positive expectation in your life. Set clear goals, create a plan of action, and take consistent steps towards your desired outcomes. Remember that your expectations are not set in stone, and that you have the power to shape your beliefs and experiences.

Finally, I want to thank you for taking the time to read this book. I hope that it has provided you with valuable insights and practical tools to transform your mindset, achieve your goals, and live your best life. Always remember that the power of expectation is within you, and that you have the ability to create the future you desire.

Thank You

As we reach the end of this book, I want to say thanks for reading this book.

I want to get this information out to as many people as possible. If you found this book helpful, I would greatly appreciate you leaving me a review. This helps others find the book as well.

Disclaimer

This document is geared towards providing exact and reliable information in regards to the topic and issue covered. The publication is sold on the idea that the publisher is not required to render an accounting, officially permitted, or otherwise, qualified services. If advice is necessary, legal, financial, medical or professional, a practiced individual in the profession should be ordered.

This information is not presented by a financial or medical practitioner and is for entertainment, educational and informational purposes only. The content is not intended as a substitute for professional medical advice, diagnosis, or treatment. Always seek the advice of your physician or other qualified health care provider with any questions you may have regarding a medical condition. Never disregard professional medical advice or delay in seeking it because of something you have read.

The information provided herein is stated to be truthful and consistent, in that any liability, in terms of inattention or otherwise, by any usage or abuse of any policies, processes, or directions contained within is the solitary and utter responsibility of the recipient reader. Under no circumstances

188

DISCLAIMER

will any legal responsibility or blame be held against the publisher for any reparation, damages, or monetary loss due to the information herein, either directly or indirectly.

www.ingramcontent.com/pod-product-compliance
Lightning Source LLC
Chambersburg PA
CBHW060516130626
46553CB00002B/522